To Sappho, My Sister

Lesbian Sisters Write About Their Lives

Lee Fleming, Editor

First published in Australia
by Spinifex Press Pty Ltd
504 Queensberry Street
North Melbourne, Vic. 3051
Australia
spinifex@peg.apc.org

First published by gynergy books
P.O. Box 2023, Charlottetown, PEI, Canada C1A 7N7

Printed in Canada

Copyright © Lee Fleming, 1995
Individual copyright to their articles is retained
by the contributors.

All rights reserved. Without limiting the rights under copyright
reserved above, no part of this publication may be reproduced,
stored in or introduced into a retrieval system, or transmitted, in
any form or by any means (electronic, mechanical, photocopying,
recording or otherwise), without prior written permission of both
the copyright owner and the above publisher of the book.

"Black Mother Woman" (excerpt) is from *Undersong: Chosen
Poems Old and New, Revised Edition* by Audre Lorde, and is
reprinted with the permission of W.W. Norton & Company, Inc.
Copyright © 1992, 1982, 1976, 1974, 1973, 1970, 1968
by Audre Lorde.

National Library of Australia Cataloguing-in-Publication data:

To Sappho, my sister: lesbian sisters write about their lives.

ISBN 1 875559 48 5

1. Lesbians. 2. Sisters. 3. Lesbianism. I. Fleming, Lee, 1957- .

305.4896643

Acknowledgements

Many women, from my immediate circle of friends and from the global lesbian and feminist network, provided assistance with this book project. I would like to thank the following: Lynn and Jan Andrews, Maria Göransson, Mary DiSalvo, Roberta Veniot, Sandra Furrer, Carolyn Gammon, Frances Rand of Australia's *Lesbians on the Loose*, the women at Spinifex Press, SisterVision Press and Women's Press (UK), Josée Belleau, Line Chamberland, Cathy Dunsford, Roz Hopkins at Cassell (UK), Arlene Mantle, Marie Robertson, Heidi Rankin, Francesca Polo and Maria Grazia Cassalia of *Towanda!* in Italy, Dorsie L. Hathaway, Tee Corinne, Eva Isaksson (list administrator of Euro-Queer), Amy Goodloe (list owner of Women Online), Marian Frances White.

As well, thank you to the women at gynergy books, including Janet Riopelle for her inspired book design and Inga Petri and Sibyl Frei for their unflagging enthusiasm for this project. A special thank you to Lynn Henry, the senior editor at gynergy books, for her patience, collaborative spirit and the superb editing skills she so willingly shared with me.

A final thank you to my sister Louise, who is also the publisher at gynergy. Her generosity, enthusiasm, sense of humour and love have made this editing project all worthwhile.

Contents

Introduction

"Sisterhood is powerful."
Robin Morgan

have always gravitated toward stories of families. This is not surprising — I come from a big family that has many stories and loves to tell them. Over the years, I've listened to and voraciously read stories about families of origin — mother-daughter stories, father-daughter stories and, more recently, stories about sisters. I have four sisters, one of whom is a lesbian, so I am hungry for information about the experiences of lesbian sisters in other communities, countries and cultures. I want to know what others think it means to be a lesbian sister.

Defining lesbian and gay family is a hot political topic these days. Sister Sledge's '70s disco hit "We Are Family (I Got All My Sisters and Me)" is still a durable dyke anthem, twenty years after it first reached the airwaves. My personal interest is in the way that we, as lesbians, are creating and expanding family. For many of us, our "family of origin" is a social construct and we want to choose our families. Yet, without understanding our own family dynamic, it can be hard to move on.

In 1991, my lesbian sister, Louise, who is also the publisher at gynergy books, decided that documenting the stories of lesbian sisters would make a worthy book project. Lynn and Jan Andrews, lesbian sisters who are also contributors to this anthology, initiated a North American information-gathering project. They designed a questionnaire, sent out a call for submissions to North American lesbian and feminist publications and attended the Michigan Womyn's Music Festival, where they held a workshop on lesbian sisters. The responses that they received were the starting point for my own editorial enquiries.

When I began work on this book in earnest, I found to my surprise that we have precious few models or archetypes of sisters from which to draw. Sisters have been largely ignored in literature. No epic or heroic stories of sisters readily spring to mind. The relationship between sisters has been left unexplored — or, at best, it has been marginalized — in mainstream film, literature and theatre. When I turned to my thesaurus for words relating to sisters or sisterhood, I found *sodality* and *sorority*. That was it. Of course, there are many words for brotherhood: *kinship, fellowship, fraternity, esprit de corps*. Although many would argue that these words are not gender specific, I cannot agree. It is only with the advent of feminism that women have taken the word *sister* and infused it with a meaning that is personal, yet universal — that of *female* solidarity and unity.

This book, then, is a first step in an exploration of the bond of lesbian sisterhood and of how we express it in our lives. It is full of personal narratives so diverse that one must read the whole book in order to get a sense of the common themes and threads. There is laughter and sadness; mutually or separately survived childhoods and families; long-standing, ongoing sisterhoods, and sisterhoods that have been ruptured and painstakingly pieced back together. The stories originated in sistertongues of English, German and Swedish. Each of the contributors (who represent eighteen sets of sisters) writes from a unique family, community and world vantage point.

Early on in the process of gathering submissions, I realized that I would have to be persistent in my search for lesbian sisters. I started by asking those around me and those in my more extended network. And, sure enough, I'd hear word of "this dyke who has a sister twenty years younger" or "this lesbian with two/three lesbian sisters"; or I'd be told that "there're these twins whose mother is a lesbian as well." But the most amazing family story I heard was from a lesbian friend in my home community. Her mother, who identifies as bisexual, has eight siblings (out of ten) who are gay, lesbian or bisexual. And of my friend's twenty-eight cousins on her mother's side, sixteen are gay or lesbian!

My informal network eventually extended to the Internet. I was amazed to learn just how developed the Dyke World Wide Web is. More lesbians are getting on-line every day, and they are sharing personal stories and experiences — many for the first time — from within this unique, instant-communication tool. I heard about or from lesbian sisters from many different parts of the world, and a couple of submissions are a result of my surfing forays on the net.

Tracking down all the leads was another matter, and I did not always succeed. The final submissions are, by design and of necessity, subjective and experiential. Perhaps someone interested in scholarly investigation will someday undertake a more comprehensive, objective study of this unique lesbian population.

Slowly, as I found sisters who committed to writing for the book, the submissions started to arrive. I was amazed by the range of experiences that emerged with each story. Many lesbian sisters had never really thought about their relationship to each other in a specific, concrete way. They were aware of its importance, but had never tried to name it or define it. For many, it just *was*. Nonetheless, there is a kind of novelty and fascination about families that contain two or more lesbian or gay members. It is, for purposes of definition, a "phenomenon." Within our extended queer communities, we imagine it with delight, as a kind of utopian perfection. In the straight world order, our lesbian personae are served up, via mainstream and pop media, to a still-surprised and unsuspecting heterosexual public. They are preoccupied with questions that do not necessarily interest us in the same way: Is lesbianism something that is passed on through the genes? Is it contagious or infectious? The discourse on the "gay gene," with all its attendant political connotations, is a recent part of this mainstream fascination.

Not surprisingly, our own stories of lesbian sisterhood reveal different, more personal sources of fascination. Some of us have stepped outside of ourselves and written from a protective distance; some of us are immersed so deeply in our experiences that we write from the inside out, together or alone. Many of us are in the midst of upheaval or healing or peacemaking. In writing our stories, we have often felt gut-wrenching emotion. For some, it has been a real struggle to commit words to paper; for still others, the words have flowed with complete ease. We've written in a variety of ways: collaboratively, separately, because of and in spite of each other! We've told our stories in autobiographical poems, prose, letters and interviews. We are complex and mean many things to each other, and, through these stories, we are reminded that there always remains an undeniable blood connection. We are from the same root, though we may live our lesbian lives differently.

The photographs that accompany each article have their own stories to tell. Together or separately, sisters searched for just the right photograph to submit. Some are from childhood and some are recent, but each one is precious and rare, signifying a larger meaning: "We have selected our images and are sending them bravely out into the world for all to see. We are showing our faces, telling our stories."

What are the prevailing influences in our lesbian lives? Family birth order is described by many as being of great importance; and the stories of twins provide an interesting counterpoint to these dynamics. As well, the immediate and larger religious, cultural and class backgrounds that surrounded us within and outside of our biological families have shaped our ongoing relationships with each other. Many of us have had to face childhood and adolescent oppression (incest, addiction, racism, disability, religious fundamentalism, family separation, homophobia, or other forces out of our childhood control), and the after-effects have often been worked out in adulthood. For some sisters, such obstacles have been a source of shared strength. For others, they still mean separation and estrangement.

All our stories show how there are currents upon currents running through families: different takes on the same events and environment; a myriad of family dynamics and complexities. Our families of origin play immense roles in our lives, and, for lesbian sisters, the struggle to define family is a constant, evolving conversation that we are having with each other.

It is important to mention the absence of many potential contributors. Many sisters had to refuse my request for their stories. They could not write for fear of revealing information about other family members, or because they were estranged and not in contact with their sister(s). For them, I hope that this book may yield some insights into the potential for healing and connecting.

Being a lesbian sister has made this my most personal editing project yet. I am looking forward to my five straight siblings reading these profiles. They are all comfortable with and respectful of me and my life. My straight sisters' adult life experiences are very different from mine — their primary partnerships are with men, mine are with women; they are mothers, I am not. We have a blood bond, and I admire and respect each one of them, but, plain and simple, we do not share the bond of lesbian sisterhood. This does not diminish them in my heart, but it means that I have a shared story with Louise that does not include them.

I am somewhat nervous to offer the book to my mother, but I love her with my whole heart and I feel more open and willing to take risks with her than ever before. She gave birth to seven children, two of whom are lesbian daughters. I want her to read this so she'll understand us better. I would also want to give my father a copy, if he were alive, but I know I'd be afraid. I wanted him to totally accept Louise and me, but it was a hard, and sometimes bitter, stretch for him — one that he couldn't entirely face, despite his deeply felt, rarely spoken love. I understand this now.

American lesbian Jill Johnston said, "Do you know what i mean when i say i'm a human being first and a woman by accident and a lesbian by preference?" As I finish this book project I have come to know that the sum of my and Louise's knowledge and experience as lesbians is more than its parts. I see part of my own face and voice in Louise. We reflect on the meaning of our blood connection through the lens of our shared lesbian lives. I have learned that lesbian sisters are sisters by accident, but that our relationships with each other are anything but accidents. Rather, they exist by choice and through hard work.

Reader, I give you this wonderful, candid book. May our stories move you and connect you, too, to an expanded understanding of sisterhood.

— *Lee Fleming,*
June 1995,
Charlottetown

Yvette Perreault,
Suzanne Perreault
and Gisele Perreault

Canada

Ursula Steck
and Eva Steck

Germany

Sharon Washington
and Sandra Washington

IRENE YOUNG

United States

Alix Dobkin
and Julie Dobkin

United States

Gillean Chase
and Janet Bianic

DEVON SIERRA

Canada

Theresa Corrigan
and Anne Corrigan

United States

Jan Andrews
and Lynn Andrews

SANDRA WHITWORTH

Canada

Anne-Marie Pedler
and Robyn Pedler

Australia

Caffyn Kelley
and Wendy Baxter

Canada

Sister

Barbara Grier
and Diane Grier

United States

Eva Borgström
and Gunnel Borgström

KERRI CORLEY

Sweden

Karin Hergl
and Christiane Hergl

Germany

Catherine Hughes
and Mikaela Hughes

Canada

Joy McBride
and Karen McBride

Canada

Lori Yetman
and Julie Yetman

Canada

Carol Camper
and Diana Andrews

Canada

Gail Hewison, Jane
Waddy and Libby Silva

Australia

Louise Fleming
and Lee Fleming

Canada

Rites

Yvette Perreault

Left: Yvette   Centre: Gisele   Right: Suzanne

The Perreault
Family's Three
Lesbians

Yvette

It's a frigid February day in Chicago. Suzanne, Gisele and I have decided to escape the cold by shopping for lingerie in Marshall Field's, the huge downtown department store. As my younger dyke sister, Gisele, parks her new four-wheel-drive Ranger, I regret that we don't have someone following us around with a video camera to record this absolutely marvellous snapshot of lesbian-sister trivia! Here we are, gently entering mid-life: me at forty-one, Suzanne at thirty-nine and Gisele at thirty-seven — the three eldest and, as far as we know, the only gay children out of eight.

We consider ourselves fortunate to claim a Prairie birthright, and our formative years were spent in small towns, living in close proximity to a large extended family. We delight in our working-class heritage and our Francophone culture, and we continue to struggle with deeply ingrained Roman Catholic beliefs. We don't have an opportunity to see each other very often — our lives have taken us far away from one another: Suz is in Vancouver, Gisele is in Chicago and I'm in Toronto. We've worked hard to get these precious five days together in Chicago so we can enjoy uninterrupted "girl talk" time. No lovers on this trip.

Now we're going to shop for lingerie befitting the three fabulous femme dykes that we are! As we enter the fifth floor of the store, I remember how I usually hate these adventures, my round body never quite fitting properly into bras and underwear. But Gisele has found a place with sizes for us — pretty underwear that actually fits. We are a formidable presence in the store — loud and laughing and not interested in being fussed over by a clerk. We inform the clerks that we'll call them if and when we need them and, until that point, to please leave us alone. We quickly arm ourselves with dozens of brightly coloured, sexy bras and panties and march off into one of the change rooms.

I love these fancy places; the dressing room is as big as my bedroom. There's a little couch, a stuffed chair, and mirrors on three walls. All of us tromp into the same room, proceed to strip down and systematically try on our piles of underwear. I relish the glimpses of bodies like mine: the same medium-sized breasts, our round bellies, our beautiful big bums and full hips, the unmistakable signs of age and gravity slowly revealing our heritage. We are saucy, tough women carrying the genes of our Prairie foremothers, who worked in the fields, harvested huge gardens and bore countless children. Watching my two sisters strut their luscious femaleness helps me feel confident — no silly comments about losing twenty pounds or about the incongruity of wearing these lacy undergarments under jeans and sweaters. We laugh, we celebrate one another as sexy beings and we encourage one another to try on something a little more outrageous and not quite so functional. We dare one another to feel beautiful and desirable. I believe my sisters when they tell me I look good in something — they know what it's like to worry about a belly and a dimpled butt. I expect them to be brutally honest: "Tell me if this looks dorky," we say as we check out how bra straps stay up under rigorous dancing and vigorous shoulder shaking. Hours later, we leave Marshall Field's with hundreds of dollars' worth of gifts to ourselves. And this time with my sisters is truly a gift; our history has not always been so amicable.

We three are so different. I am the eldest, the cautious "good girl" who grew up anxious to please Mom and Dad, determined to follow the religious instruction of the priest and nuns who taught us. We moved a lot when I was young, my father looking for work on construction sites. I was a kid who tried to figure out the "rules" of the many new towns we moved to, always trying to fit in. I was desperate for the guidance of an older sibling. I believed it was my

TO SAPPHO, MY SISTER

job to be as "grown up" and responsible as possible, to help Mom keep order in a busy house filled with kids and always a baby in diapers. My parents are great people. Home was not scary or violent and we grew up assured that we were loved and wanted. But poverty created stress. I knew Mom and Dad worried about paying bills and the family often faced scarcity. We managed with hand-me-downs, homemade clothes, and a single tiny present for Christmas and birthdays. We were all taught to cook, clean, sew and "make do" with little. We maintain that resourcefulness as adults. But it wasn't poverty that I found most difficult; what I truly hated were those many early moves. As a little girl, even a move across town necessitated building new friendship networks. However, moving a lot definitely strengthened our sibling connections. Often we were the only people we knew, which forced us to learn to play together and sort out our differences to avoid being desperately isolated.

I was not quite two when Suzanne was born and, until then, I had enjoyed being the spoiled only child of devoted parents. The arrival of a sibling was a profound shake-up for me. She was not to be a playmate but a rival! Right from the start, Suz was different. She came into the world howling and hasn't really stopped! At the time, Mom was suffering from what we now believe was "post-partum depression" and she became emotionally unavailable for a significant length of time. I definitely wasn't happy about no longer being the centre of attention, and my toilet training suddenly became a thing of the past. I remember actively wishing Suz "gone" many times. In my perception, Suzanne was the loud kid, the "bad kid," the one who didn't care what the rules were. Instead, she made her own way into the world, as blustery and boisterous as she needed to be to create a space for herself. She was constantly bombarded by Mom and Dad and our teachers with: "Why can't you be more like your sister Yvette?" I was the one who, as a young teenager, played the organ in church, while Suzanne was the girl who got caught kissing boys behind the church!

We were forced to share a bedroom while growing up — Mom and Dad conceded to our constant bickering by giving us twin beds but we were told to negotiate the rest on our own. We drew a line down the centre of the room, divided the closet and dresser space exactly in half, and defined separate areas of the bedroom as "mine" and off limits. We still tell numerous stories about our ongoing pranks: the stolen clothes, make-up, jewellery, boyfriends, the screaming fights ... there was always a competitive, angry tone between us. It took us a long while to see that we played out different aspects of a whole person by dividing into the good daughter and the rebellious daughter. Years of personal therapy have led each of us to appreciate the traits of the other within ourselves. It was only when I learned about the rebellious parts of me that I could celebrate Suzanne's unique characteristics.

Suzanne and I always knew that Mom and Gisele had a special connection. We could sense that Mom was a more relaxed and ready parent at that stage of her life. We nicknamed Gisele "Buddha Baby" for her roly-poly body and funny grin. She was a tough, likable kid with an opinion of her own about everything. She was neither the "good girl" nor the "bad girl" (those roles were already taken) and could confidently become "herself." Gisele had the benefit of being born into the family when the anxiety-provoking moves were less frequent. My parents were slowly becoming more stable. Suz and I both paved the way into school systems and friendship networks. By the time Gisele was born, I had resigned my four-year-old self to the fact that I was never going to be an "only" child, so my role was going to be one of "good little mother's helper" (meaning "bossy big sister"). I found Gisele easier to relate to than Suzanne and we often played together. We were not quite best companions, because a four-year age difference is a lot when you're a kid, but neither were we competitors.

After Gisele's birth, other kids followed: Claude, Denise, Daniel, Louis and Joel. Four girls and four boys in all — a busy, chaotic family that fit well into the small Francophone Prairie towns loaded with our cousins, aunts and uncles, and grandmothers. By all standards, we grew up "normal," with a good mix of boyfriends and girlfriends. I can't remember consciously meeting a lesbian or gay man during my teen years. The topic of homosexuality was never discussed at the dinner table. I didn't know that people *could* be gay. Although we never talked about this until later in life, all three of us eldest girls had "special girlfriends" with whom we first experimented with kissing and fondling; boys came later. Each of us also had extensive heterosexual experience, but we didn't settle with that life choice. I often wonder how much heartache we might have spared ourselves if we had known about lesbianism as an option during our sexual awakenings.

I came out first. I was sent away to a convent in the late '60s to complete my high-school education. I suspect my family thought

I'd make a good nun. I lasted a year, and beyond the confines of St. Lazare, I encountered a world of social and political upheaval: everything was changing. I began to challenge the Church's rules about sex, to question my predestined role of either the convent or marriage and motherhood. I was a confused teenager; I knew I wanted more from life than what a small town offered. My parents were nervous about me "spreading my wings." Having no role models or mentors to help me create new possibilities was the most difficult aspect of being the eldest — I acted as the groundbreaker for the rest of the kids and had to live with my own mistakes.

Right after high school, I left home to go into psychiatric nursing. I was dating a nice boyfriend who taught me about tender, fun sex, but our birth-control methods were primitive and I ended up pregnant at eighteen. Everyone expected me to get married and raise the child, but all of me rebelled. The man was nice enough, but boring. I didn't know what else was out there, but it surely had to be more than this. I agonized over the decision, but gave the baby up for adoption and hitchhiked to Vancouver to start a new life.

Somehow that act of defiance opened doors into choices other than marriage and motherhood. Although my intimate relationships with men were more or less satisfying, I was certainly looking for "more." Still, it was a complete shock when, at twenty, I found myself falling head over heels in love with a woman! The sex was fantastic and passionate, and the relationship tumultuous. Judy's feminist analysis helped put my life into perspective — I wasn't crazy; there was something wrong with the way society gave women limited options. I describe the combination of great sex and feminist perspective as "coming home." Not only did I feel good about myself, but as a lesbian feminist I now had a mission — to change society's view of women and of homosexuality. I loved being a dyke.

That burgeoning pride reshaped not only my identity but also my way of relating to my family. No longer did I feel ashamed of myself as the sinner/slut who had run away from home. I didn't choose to come out to Mom and Dad right away, but I began to write long letters home, arguing about the role of women in society. I was paving the way for later news about my own new role in society. I did come out to my siblings. I recall hosting a party in Winnipeg when I visited with my lover Judy. Suzanne and Gisele were specifically invited to the party, and I felt secure in talking openly with them about my choice to be a lesbian. They were curious: "How do you know when you're a lesbian?" "Does this mean you hate men?" "What's the sex like?" "Mom and Dad are going to flip out ..." Bringing them news of my lesbian identity was a crucial turning point in our relationship — it symbolized the shift from sibling rivalry to the creation of new bonds as young adults. I was no longer simply their big sister, "miss goodie-goodie."

Shortly after coming out to my siblings, I returned to life in Vancouver and moved in with Judy. Gisele called one afternoon to say she was leaving home and coming to Vancouver. Although I wasn't enamoured with the idea of keeping up the big-sister role, I gave Gisele a place to stay for a while and helped her get set up in the city. I certainly wasn't prepared for the evening Gisele came to me and told me that she thought she was a lesbian. I was stunned; she didn't even have a girlfriend! It had taken me the turmoil of crazily falling in love with a woman to actually believe I could be a lesbian, and here was my "kid sister" taking to this identity like a duck to water. I don't think I made it easy. Gisele was seventeen years old. She was too young for the bars — whatever would happen to her? I knew her coming-out process would be painful; how do you come out when no one wants to sleep with you because you're jail bait? I doubted her new-found identity because, after all, she hadn't actually had sex with a woman yet. Maybe this just looked good because she had had several bad relationships with men?

I didn't exactly throw Gisele a coming-out party when she began her journey into the lesbian community. In fact, I suspect I made it tough for her. I told her to find her own way, and "make sure you are doing this because it is right for you, not because you are following in my footsteps." And somehow Gisele did it. Her first few sexual relationships were disasters, but that didn't deter her. Eventually, I could see that her lesbian identity was something central to her being: she certainly identified as a dyke even without being in sexual relationships — unlike me, who had to be firmly in a relationship and getting all the "goodies" in order to balance the "shame and shit" of a heterosexist world. I still have such respect for Gisele's determination and her clarity about knowing what was right for her.

In the meantime, Suzanne, Claude and Denise had also moved to Vancouver. While we saw one another from time to time, they were the "het contingent" of the sibling connection, and Gisele and I kept some distance. We were all busy constructing our own adult lives and were occupied with jobs, friendships, relationships, hobbies and various political pursuits. We remained connected but not overly intimate. Having one other dyke sister who understood my feelings of being "left out" of family gatherings and removed from parental recognition was extremely validating. I'm not sure I could have maintained the anti-homophobia education I relentlessly pursued with my straight siblings without Gisele's support. We unconsciously seemed to take turns — if I was frustrated by the hets "not getting it," Gisele was there to pick up the ball while I stepped back and renewed my spirit.

Gisele and I continued to thrive in the lesbian community in Vancouver, although both of us made our own way. We lived in a communal house for a period of time, but that was not a satisfying living arrangement — there were too many struggles with our respective lovers and too much old sibling rivalry, and not enough skills in conflict resolution to sort out those differences. So we lived apart and moved in different circles. I worked for a feminist organization as a counsellor and a community organizer. Gisele moved in the arts community, involved herself in theatre and radio, and became an artist in her own right, creating works in stained glass and leather. I envied her artistic flair; my own work with people did not always feel satisfying and the results seemed far less concrete.

After five years of calling ourselves "lesbian," and building open, strong, supportive relationships with our straight siblings, Gisele and I decided it was time to tell Mom and Dad who we really were. The secret was hard for the other kids to maintain — our family prided itself on real communication, from the heart with no bullshit. We had not told Mom and Dad prior to this for very good reasons — we knew the doctrines of the Catholic Church would impede our parents from easily accepting us and we were terrified of losing whatever intimacy we had with them. Even if we weren't talking about everything of importance in our lives, at least we hadn't been shut out of the family. But eventually Gisele and I were at an impasse with Mom and Dad — either we took a risk and moved forward or we cut off communication. The latter was an unacceptable option. We made a decision to come out jointly to them the next time the family was visiting Vancouver; it would have to be done face to face.

We developed a strategy involving the co-operation of all the kids in the family. Gisele and I were going to take Mom and Dad out for dinner toward the end of their visit and, during a conversation over coffee at my apartment, we would tell them about our lesbianism.

Yvette Perreault, Suzanne Perreault, Gisele Perreault   11

The task of the straight siblings was to take care of our parents the next day. We knew they would need a lot of support and we correctly believed there was little chance they would get it from the parish priest. It was a painful night for all of us — Gisele had decided to come out first, as she suspected Mom and Dad would think she was only following in my footsteps if I came out first. (Of course they thought this anyway, but we tried!) Gisele and I were both very public dykes, which added to the look of panic in Mom and Dad's eyes. Not for us a quiet, closeted, suburban gay life. Gisele worked on a weekly lesbian radio show and I was in the process of publishing my first book on lesbianism and feminism. Our parents' reaction was predictably one of shock and protest: "Why do you have to call yourselves lesbians? Couldn't you just live like that and not tell anyone? Why did you have to tell us?"

It was wonderful to know Mom and Dad could take their pain and confusion directly to their other children, who were more or less understanding of our choices. It took our parents a lot of time and prayer to make their own decision to get to know us for all of who we are and to accept our partners as more than just "friends." The tolerance and ongoing acceptance of our own siblings made it possible for Mom and Dad to talk to people who could counteract the messages from the church and community. It also provided them with role models — people who challenged their own internalized homophobia. When Mom and Dad had difficulties, our siblings were there to gently prod them toward changing their attitudes and behaviours, arguing that we, too, should be allowed to sleep in the same bed as our partners when visiting, and encouraging Mom to include photos of our lovers in the "Family Gallery" on the living-room wall.

We were a family with two lesbians. We were all adjusting rather well to this fact when Suzanne began a hot affair with a woman.

Like me, Suzanne had left home early, moving from Winnipeg to Toronto and finally settling into Vancouver for a stretch. Hers had not been a happy adolescence. She had become involved with a violent man and left him only after a serious suicide attempt. It was hard for us to reach her. She maintained communication primarily with our youngest sister, Denise, and not at a "heart" level with her dyke sisters. I think moving to Vancouver saved Suzanne's life. She began living with a good man and established a sweet, tender relationship. Given Suzanne's "wild girl" history, neither Gisele nor I was particularly surprised when we heard that she was having an affair with a dyke whom we both knew. But it did create political dilemmas for us: Suzanne began to define herself as bisexual, a term with little acceptance in the lesbian community of the late '70s. How would we deal with her in our friendship circles? Did we integrate her into lesbian-only events? Was she getting the benefits of our hard-won safety in community without doing any of the work? Was she getting the "goodies" of being with women without taking on any of the struggles of lesbian identity? We were not in familiar territory, and neither were there role models in our family for Suzanne's type of sexual identity, but Suz continued for years to quietly describe herself as bisexual.

It wasn't until Suzanne and I moved to Montreal in the early '80s that we truly began to "be friends." We finally had some things in common: we shared the isolation of assimilated Francophones from the Prairies living in Quebec and we were both in transition from relationship break-ups. I found myself turning to Suzanne for comfort, bringing her my confusion and distress. And I found her to be a wise, funny, playful, joyous woman. It had never occurred to me that she could be such a source of support, but, alone in Montreal, we overcame years of competition. I cherish those memories of our time together in our tiny, cold walk-ups in Montreal and my surprise at Suzanne's strength of character and compassion. All these years, I had imagined her to be so busy being the rebellious one that she was unable to listen, let alone have wise opinions. I suspect she had imagined me to be so busy being the caretaker/counsellor that I wasn't needy and vulnerable. To experience each other differently was a significant turning point in our relationship.

A year later, we both moved to Toronto. I had a new lover and was settling into a women's housing co-operative and a new job. Suzanne was living with us as she settled into Toronto. She had firmly said good-bye to her last male partner and was beginning a relationship with a woman in Toronto. Her bisexual identity still troubled me deeply. I wrote her a long letter asking her to consider identifying as a lesbian now that she was no longer with a man. Could she see her way to taking on the full weight of a lesbian identity now that she was in fact living as a lesbian? If, down the road, she chose to love a man again, then we'd deal with that. I'm not so certain now why that clarity of identity was so important to me ... but it was at the time. I'm sure that our history had influenced her long-standing decision to remain "bisexual"; the old phrase

"Why can't you be more like Yvette?" surely had been playing in her memory. For whatever reason, Suzanne began her new life in Toronto calling herself a lesbian.

Just as I had done with Gisele, I helped introduce Suzanne into the women's community, but Suzanne quickly developed her own style. She moved into the housing co-op with a new lover and soon created a lively friendship network. Suzanne is a social, gregarious creature who loves night life. She and I spent a lot of time together — talking, hanging out, struggling in our housing co-op, throwing dinner parties at the house, dressing up and hitting the bars, being a fun-femme presence at the women's dances and, most important, being part of each other's life transitions. It was a huge loss for me when Suzanne, her lover of many years and her best friend left Toronto and moved back to the West Coast. We had become great friends. The many years of fighting were over.

Eight years went by and, although Suzanne was still living as a lesbian, she was not out to Mom and Dad. This began to create complications for us. With Suzanne not able to share details about her life, Mom and Dad worried about her, imagining that she had a lonely existence of work, interior-decorating school and a few friends. They believed that her most intimate relationship was with her cat! Gisele and I didn't exactly encourage Suzanne to reveal herself to Mom and Dad. We had already suffered through a few difficult years with them and could finally talk to them with minimal tension. To introduce another lesbian into the family would trigger their pain and we quietly feared we'd all be back at square one. I was certain I'd get the blame for this, too, and Suzanne's worst fear was that Mom and Dad wouldn't recognize lesbianism as her choice but rather see her as unduly influenced by Gisele and me. I remember telling Suzanne, "Be sure you're *really* a lesbian before you come out" — a fancy way of both criticizing her bisexual stance and telling her I was unprepared to actively support her in coming out. Eventually, though, there was little for her to lose and a lot to gain by coming out. She lacked the supportive communication we had with our parents and we all knew it. We were also tired of covering up for her and evading any direct questions about Suzanne's life.

Suzanne decided to come out by using a different approach from Gisele's and mine. She wrote a long coming-out letter to Mom and Dad, which Gisele and I were invited to edit. Once again, all the kids were poised, ready to support both our parents and our sister. Suz expected the same type of instant rejection and horror we had received, but we were all pleasantly surprised: Mom and Dad were exceptionally good with Suz — happy that she had talked with them, pleased that she did indeed have a broad range of interests, a lover and a rich friendship circle. Now Suzanne is in the process of building "real," open relationships with both Mom and Dad. It's a relief to all of us, although I admit to pangs of jealousy that my own coming out to Mom and Dad wasn't so immediately supported. Gisele's and my efforts with our parents were apparent in their response to Suzanne's announcement, so I do take pride in that.

Openness seems to beget more openness. Mom and Dad grew tired of keeping secrets from their own family members; it was becoming increasingly difficult for them to talk about the exploits of their three eldest daughters because so much of our lives were connected to lesbian experiences. So Mom and Dad courageously "came out" to their own immediate family members through an open letter to their brothers and sisters, announcing the fact that they have lesbian daughters and telling our aunts and uncles a little about our lives. The response has been guarded but okay. My very conservative, extremely religious uncle Ed said to me, "If your mother and father can accept you so lovingly, then so can I." Mom and Dad's willingness to come out as parents of lesbians has helped us establish a more meaningful relationship with our extended family. Their act has reconnected us to our Prairie roots.

Moving into mid-life, I feel so honoured to have dyke sisters. I love my het siblings, but there is a level of "soul-sharing" possible with someone who shares similar life experiences — it provides a shorthand for communication and enables us to offer quick support in hard times because we truly know each other's lives. We live thousands of miles apart and I am often saddened by that reality. Gisele is with her lover in Chicago and is now an American citizen. She continues to work as an artist and is becoming increasingly known for her mask work and stained glass. She and Peggy have bought a house and it looks like they'll be in the States for a long while to come. Suzanne has just bought a house in Vancouver with an ex-lover and a best friend. They're working things out and it looks like she'll be there for the foreseeable future. And I'm settled here in Toronto — still with Debbie after thirteen years and still in the housing co-op. We've recently bought a little cabin on a lake in Madoc, so we're putting down roots here. But I deeply miss the day-to-day relationship I had with my sisters. We have to work harder to maintain our intimacy with all the complexities of time, distance and separate lives.

I *am* conscious of the intimacy and connection I share with Suz and Gisele, though — even without the benefits of daily contact. I am better in the world when I am "clear and connected" with my sisters. We talk often, in long phone calls during which we discuss the details of each other's lives, projects, relationships, struggles. There is rarely a decision or argument or hard place in my life that I experience without processing it with either Suz or Gisele. There are times of lesser/greater connection, but the web is alive. We talk "real," we tell each other about our dreams, we take care of one another. We have hired a therapist to work with us as a group when we've been in a conflict with one another. We *make* time to be together — time like the Chicago underwear trip. We delight in our similarities and explore the differences. Birth order was a challenge, and we'll probably be struggling with that forever. But anything seems possible with our commitment to "work it through." We've had to allow for our many differences — we've made different choices in life work, we hold different political views, we communicate differently. Still, it is better to be talking about those "gaps" than not. Times when we've been separated through unresolved conflict have felt excruciating. The heart-sustaining moments come when we call on each other in times of life crisis, and respond by getting on a plane and offering love and concrete, physical support. I wonder what delights and turmoil the next forty years will bring this family that has been blessed with three dyke sisters!

Left: Yvette   Centre: Gisele   Right: Suzanne

Alix Dobkin
and Julie Dobkin

Left: Julie   Right: Alix

"We Didn't Get It Easy, but We Got It"

Title on previous page taken from "Talking Lesbian," by Alix Dobkin, on the album, *Lavender Jane Loves Women*, Women's Wax Works, A001, copyright 1973.

etween the time Alix and i agreed to contribute to this anthology and the time we actually started writing our pieces, our very sweet and beloved Pop died. His death had a lot to do with the great and amazing transformation which now allows us to be close as sisters. Before this past year, Alix had always put up walls between us. I'd been open to Alix and had waited for her to change — sometimes patiently, often not. Then, a few years ago — in one of our rare, painful and awkward relationship-processing discussions — Alix acknowledged that the walls were, in fact, her doing. I didn't get that she cared whether they were up or not; i might have from her expression and the fact that she was engaging in the conversation, but i was still seeing her as i always had — as satisfied with herself and not needing me to be included as a part of her inner circle. And, although that conversation has played a small part in bringing her walls down, i'd always known and felt that things wouldn't really change until she became more self-examining and faced the pain that our shadow side always holds. During the last three years or so, while performing the Amazonian task of writing her memoirs, Alix has looked at her life and at our family life as she never had before.

I know that i've had my own personal growing to do, as well. I believe our old patterns couldn't have been replaced until i become more self-assured and grounded in the material sense. So here we are, with connections and bonds forged through fire. I hope, as i know Alix does, that our story will at least be of interest — and will perhaps inspire — other sisters/siblings to do the work necessary to find those deeper, loving places that are hidden by misplaced anger and blame.

— Julie Dobkin

Left: Julie   Right: Alix

Alix

Dear Julie,

It shouldn't surprise us that we have become so much closer since Pop died and left the elder generation of our family in our hands. We did pretty well together during that week in September, when we went through his stuff, making decisions about what to do with it all — especially considering how he held the centre in place for everyone, and how sad we are that, for the first time in our lives, we're without his comforting, rock-solid presence. Becoming hysterical while reading those goofy old letters together was tremendous fun, and healing too, I think. It's always good to laugh, especially when the going is rough.

I'm glad we discovered that letter with my teenaged complaint about "not feeling included in the family"; it's proof that you were not the only one, and that I, too, was capable of feeling bad about myself and harbouring suspicions that I was not worthy. You know, I'm used to putting on a good front because I thought that Mom and Pop counted on it and because it's generally the truth of my spirits; the result of studied optimism and a deliberate upbeat attitude. After all, as

Ralph Nader says, "There's no payoff for pessimism" (or words to that effect). I whole-heartedly believe that.

But there are times when only a thin line separates a healthy, positive approach, on the one hand, and pretense and denial or "wooden-headedness"— as Barbara Tuchman characterizes "folly" — on the other. I've probably stepped over that line on more than a few occasions, in my enthusiasm to achieve and to be thought of as capable or "good." It's the down and defensive side of my invincible act, I know, and it often makes me unapproachable. I put up a front that I always have to be equal to the task — or appear to be equal to it — and that's something you've had to make your way around. And you still have to deal with it sometimes, because I haven't gotten over it and, at fifty-four, I most likely never will get over it entirely. I'm not even sure where to start, how much is real, or who I'd be without it, et cetera.

Pop's death has most likely been hardest on you, the youngest. The generational gap you have suddenly bridged is the widest. It is less wide for me, since in some ways I have felt like a responsible adult ever since Carl made me an older sister at age six. Three years later you were born, putting a point on it. It's the old first-child-being-the-responsible-one syndrome, which leads, no doubt, to the roots of our relationship problems. Carl reached his age of relative independence before you did, yet was too young to assume any of the child-care responsibility for you. You still needed looking after. My first job was to keep one, then two, little kids occupied in the mornings while Mom got herself together. It was a job I did not relish, to say the least.

It never occurred to me how much harder it was for you, at five years of age, than for me at fourteen, or even Carl at eight, when Mom went back to school. It wasn't your fault that I, your big sister, was supposed to take charge of you when Mom was unavailable. I was, as usual, completely wrapped up in myself and my own life, which was either utterly miserable or ecstatically busy. In either case, I know that my interests generally lay outside the family, and that I spent time with you because I had to. Not the best foundation for a relationship.

Who knows how much time I spent looking after you? My sense, rather than any clear memory, tells me that it was a lot, but that's probably an exaggeration, since it was a chore I performed reluctantly, always wanting to be somewhere else. You, little Julie, were not old enough to hold up your end of a satisfying conversation, yet demanded my attention when I felt like I had better places for it.

My gut reaction toward you was established during those early years and it originated from the expectation that I had to be where I didn't want to be. I also resented the pressure to be the grown-up. Ever since then, anything suggesting babyish behaviour from you drives me up a wall, to the point where, sometimes, even routine acknowledgement of your feelings — good and bad alike — immediately provokes my emotional distance.

At the same time that I feel connected to you and care about your well-being, my love for you has been intercepted by a frustrating resentment and the heaviness attending my sisterly obligations. I withdrew for many years, at a loss about how to improve my bad attitude and how to deal with my bad feelings without hurting yours. When we were together, I'd take a deep breath and try not to scowl at you like I did back in Lynnewood Gardens when you were a toddler and I was an unhappy, impatient babysitter in training.

Later, as a young mother, having to keep two-year-old Adrian quiet and amused while others slept revived all the ancient crankiness and resentment. I hated it so much. That residue had been waiting for over two decades to hit me like a ton of bricks, and I was absolutely stunned by it until I began to make some connections between my feelings for you and for Adrian. They go so deep that I still confuse your name with Adrian's when all three of us are together. I always have to think and sort out who is who before opening my mouth. You may have noticed this!

As our age difference diminishes in importance, we have worked to build a friendship as more equal adults. But there is no denying that childhood imprinting and the toll it has taken on our relationship. Those grooves in the youthful brain run deep, and we've spent many years working to undo and replace them with happier and more compatible ones, trying to find and create new and common ground.

Given the differences in years and temperament between us — and the miles between us — I think we've been doing pretty well, especially in the last decade, and more especially in the last year. And perhaps now, with both parents gone, we'll be able to move ahead. Life, after all, goes on, and so must we.

But it's been a tearful road up to now, with anguish enough for both of us; and there's no one, including Mom, with her own suffering heart, to blame for it. We each understand and experience our own version of deep, non-verbal heartbreak, which is passed on and lessened, it seems, through our female line. And we each deal with it differently: Grandma through her denial and fortitude; Mom with her martyrdom, her silent, courageous dignity and supreme acts of faith in herself.

No two objects can occupy the identical space, and neither can sisters. As a consequence, our individual identities and styles are worlds apart. This becomes obvious in our artwork, which is a family custom I established and you carry on — proof positive of effective big-sistership and a tradition we can both be proud of. Pop certainly was proud of it. How typical that I majored in oil painting and that my art is controlled, disciplined and representational, while you work, freely and imaginatively — and often abstractly — in watercolours.

We have separate spheres of influence and knowledge. I am an educator (I like to think) and entertainer; you are a healer and artist. Both are professions true to our family ideals and the natural result of how we were raised in the world. Your expertise in health- and body-related subjects certainly exceeds mine, and I like to learn various facts and benefit from the tips you dispense. You're getting better at it too. I'm grateful for your advice on my posture, which I constantly remind myself of, and your helpful discussion of why I slouch whereas Mom's and Grandma's backs were perfectly straight. I think you really know your stuff, and I'm more than happy to let you keep that lead.

Naturally, I'm delighted that you eventually came out because it was so important to my life and because I think being a Lesbian is terrific. It gives me great pleasure to inform people that my sister's a dyke, and I love speaking the same language as you, with the same references and assumptions that neither of us has to explain or omit.

Although Adrian isn't a Lesbian, she is an offspring of our community, where, as you know, she feels quite at home. We three are equally and uniquely blessed, as family and as individuals within a common tribe. We each recognize and appreciate this, in addition to recognizing the dues we pay, and have paid, for the privilege.

To me, us both being Lesbians means that we have more than a passing interest in each other's lives; that we owe each other our best, most authentic behaviour, and that we are responsible for how we treat each other. Sharing positive expectations, values and beliefs as part of a tribe is a good way to spend a life; in our case, it is an outstanding way to live, given that we were raised in a progressive family. I consider us extremely lucky to be able to carry on the best of our extraordinary family strengths within a common community. A double dose of Dobkins for Lesbian Nation can only be a plus. "Good, the values" (to paraphrase our great grandma's version of "grace" at the table, "Good, the food").

I don't remember when you came out, because I had been aware of your close and loving relationships (complex, as only Lesbian ones can be) with Nadya (and Linda) for years, and the date blurs in my memory. I thought you probably were one, but I couldn't be sure. I know I thought you should be, and in thinking about it now I have to reflect on my big-sister modelling — how unconscious the modelling was and how hard it must have been for you to stake your own ground outside my shadow.

It isn't easy, even in the best of circumstances, for younger sisters to find their own path in the wake of an overachieving, go-getting older one. Toward that end, you deserve lots of credit for making your own way across the continent to find your own space. It was a positive but difficult and risky move, and I am extremely happy for your success in finding independent ground on which to stand. I know you had a tough time acknowledging your own Lesbian identity, in your own right, in your own way. Of course, you did it in your own time; unfortunately for you, that time had to be after I had done it first, publicly and dramatically. It must have taken you a huge amount of thought and "sorting out," when *Lavender Jane* was a kind of national Lesbian standard and I had the ownership of "Lesbian," at least in our family. It wasn't an easy act to follow, and even I'm not always successful at it.

Our parents were progressive, accepting of us and always loving, but there was no way to predict their response to a second Lesbian daughter. I don't envy your position or the confusion and conflict you must have felt about that. Not wanting to add to Mom's or-deal with cancer must have been gruesome, as well, and you have my belated sympathy, for what it's worth. I'm sure I wasn't much help to you from my distant, lofty and often judgmental heights, and I wish I had known then what I know now. But don't we all? Don't we wish we could talk to Mom, ask her the questions we are wise enough to think of now, fill in the gaps growing less accessible by the hour, get the closure with her that will never happen? It is too sad.

On the other hand, we were all able to appreciate how much better Pop's death was than Mom's, and how much more satisfaction there was with and for him, fifteen years later. He was very proud of, and happy with, each of us, and he wasn't shy about letting us know it. That's pretty good, and we're pretty lucky to have had this father and this family to grow up in. The latest generation of Dobkins promises that the good fortune will survive and increase, and that the best of our traditions will live on long after us.

I'm really glad that we are in the same family, Julie. It couldn't be otherwise, and I look forward to hearing your take on all this. Maybe the best is truly yet to come for us and our loved ones. It could happen.

Congratulations to Nadya on the new job. Kiss the doggie, have an easy move and a wonderful New Year, and don't forget to send me the card you made for the occasion. Lots of love to you all ... especially you!

Stay well,
Alix.

Julie

Dear Lex,

I feel that if i knew how to begin, the rest of this response would magically unfold. It's more than a little daunting to sort out my thoughts and feelings about us. There's so much more love and caring now, and, until recently, there's been such a lot of resentment and hurt and anger. But maybe i'm giving it too much importance. After all, i've been thinking about writing you a letter for around thirty years. I was fifteen. I know you remember that Thanksgiving weekend when i stayed with you on Barrow Street in the Village. That was the only time i can remember us simply hanging out. We had fun, and you showed me around your life there. I know it was a chemically induced exception. You were still flying from that superdelic trip, and i guess it allowed you to suspend your usual judgment of me. In any event, i was thrilled to feel like i finally had a sister. You turned me on to pot for the first time that weekend and took me to hear two new folk-rock acts — Danny Kalb and the Blues Project and Richie Havens — at the Night Owl. You even introduced me to Odetta. I figured the reason for your newfound interest in me was that rock-and-roll had just become "hip" to the folk world (this being 1964, and the Beatles had changed everything), and here i was, an authentic source for the latest rock-and-roll and dances. I felt like a real specimen — but if that meant i was included in your life, that was okay by me.

Not too many weeks after that mind-blowingly exceptional weekend, you called home to Philly to tell Mom and Pop that you were going to marry Sam. I got off the extension after hearing you break the news to Mom, went into my room and cried my eyes out. I was sure our newfound friendship was over, and i was right. You resumed being the distant and judgmental sister you had been before that weekend. But now that i knew it was possible for you to enjoy my company, i thought of writing you a letter that would reveal my true being, so you would somehow see me and not that awful, needy little girl you projected onto me most of the time. I knew that's what you did, but i never understood why — not until you told me about your caretaking of Carl and me. You said you hadn't remembered it yourself until Selma (Mom's friend from childhood) told you about it. That was only a relatively few years ago, and it was the most helpful single piece of our puzzle. I have zero memory of you taking care of me. In fact, when i got your letter, i made an entry in my journal listing all the memories of you i had prior to my teens. I think there were eight memories on the list, and they were either pleasant or interesting. After that, most of what i remember is how i felt put down whenever we were together, or how i felt like a puppy hanging around, grateful for a few little pats on the head, a few interested words.

It's not like we never had anything to talk about; there was family stuff, and, later, lesbian news and gossip. And, after that, there was always you and your career. But when those subjects were exhausted, it was like falling off a cliff — there was nowhere to go and we would descend into an uncomfortable silence. It always reminded me of the moment that follows the punchline, "So, if you had a brother, would he like noodles?"

Of course, it's not a coincidence that this exchange, this project in which we're participating, consists of my responding to something you've initiated. You were approached for this anthology because of who you are in the world. I have no problem with that. *Au contraire*, i've always been extremely proud of your career and have almost never minded being called "Alix Dobkin's sister." It's opened some doors for me, your name. There have been countless interesting, often valuable, conversations i've had with strangers and acquaintances that would not have happened otherwise. Many of my good friends and precious connections have come from being a worker at the Michigan Womyn's Music Festival — and, therefore, from you.

Just as important, though, is the fact that while i've spent most of my life feeling both unseen and unheard by you, i've wanted, at times almost desperately, for us to be close and confiding sisters. As i grew up and realized i wasn't going to have that, i attempted to salvage my pride by trying not to express anything that might make you reject me — which is to say, nothing that had to do with what i felt or thought or anything i wanted from you, unless it was about you. Being the emotional and sensitive creature that i am, there is no way i could succeed at hiding my feelings entirely. I just did the best i could to maintain a semblance of dignity around you.

It's true that we began to breach the enormous gap between us after i came out as a lesbian. It's also true that your being the "definitive dyke" (my term at the time) made it extremely hard for me to come out as a lesbian after being a bisexual for more than ten years. I was angry, because i knew that, if and when i did come out as a lesbian, you *would* be more accepting of me. I was disgusted that you were so disapproving of my wearing a denim skirt. I couldn't believe you couldn't see me for who i was rather than what i was or what i was wearing, to say nothing of how much your separatism offended me — and Mom and Pop. They saw it as the same kind of mistake they had made by being in the Party — preaching to the converted and being insular. I was more put off by the amount of time you and your friends spent putting men down and by your generally arrogant attitude.

So, yes, it took me a while to come out on my own. Your existence wasn't a decisive factor in my becoming entirely lesbian. I needed time to get men out of my system. I think it was a kind of socialized addiction. What really did it was Linda saying to me: "Julie, shit or get off the pot!" At the time, it seemed obvious to me that being a lesbian would allow me to have more integrity as a woman and a feminist. (The then-new/now-old adage: "Feminism is the theory, lesbianism the practice.") It may have felt like a choice then, but it hasn't for a long time. (It's reassuring to think that almost all of our cells are replaced every seven years — now all of me has been lesbian more than twice.) I remember having a conversation in which i came out to Soph (Mom's best friend) and she implied that i was just emulating you. What a laugh, i thought.

I never did come out to Mom as a lesbian, but she knew how important my relationship to Nadya was. After all, we'd been together for two years before Mom died. She and Pop were a lot more accepting and inclusive of Nadya than you were until just a few years ago. My coming out to Pop happened kind of inadvertently. We were walking down Essex Street, doing our usual Lower East Side jaunt, and the subject of your performing exclusively in women-only space came up. I was defending the need for it, and he was saying something to the effect that only separatists wanted women-only space. I yelled out, "Well, i'm a lesbian and i'm not a separatist, and i need women-only space, too!" So that was that. I did have to work on him regularly to get him to believe that i didn't hate men in the same way that you did. I pointed out to him that most of his friends were women, and that the probable reasons for this were related to our choices to be lesbians. After a time, he accepted that you and i were different kinds of lesbians.

The difference between us now is less than it was then, but it seemed enormous at the time. I've been agonizing over whether i would even be able find the vocabulary of a shared language with which to write, to communicate what i've kept myself from revealing all those years. I've even had a bad dream where, because i am somewhat critical in this letter, you were pissed off at me and we lost our newfound ease with each other. I remember, in years past, trying to talk to you about some of my internal struggles and you just didn't understand. It was so confusing, because all the other women in my life seemed to know just what i was talking about. It's still hard for me to reconcile my image of you, as the one who always did what you wanted and had everyone's approval, with the young girl i know now you were, who felt unworthy and excluded. But i find it a relief that you can share your vulnerability with me.

I can hardly begin to imagine us attempting this dialogue prior to this last year. It took as extreme a circumstance as Pop's death to bring us closer. I think it happened as it did because you needed me to be a strong, aware and capable woman, one who could hold her own in a situation that was tough for you, too. As for myself, i don't know how i could have made it through this devastating grief without your warmth, caring and sensitivity. More than anything, i wish to create a deeper friendship between us. The fact that others will read this letter changes nothing except some of the external form and the timing. I figure that if i can actually communicate to you, to my satisfaction, how i've felt for all these years, that will be sufficient. *Dayenu*. It is possible to do this at all because, in your letter to me, you were obviously as open and as self-examining as i've ever known you to be.

In the process of thinking about and discussing this response, i've achieved an understanding that's led to a kind of catharsis. It has to do with you being the one who was there instead of Mom. Clearly, you'd received some of the rage i understandably felt toward Mom — a typical childhood act, to protect the parent from being judged deficient. This i'd come to understand in therapy, where i spent many more hours concerned with our relationship (yours and mine) than with anything else. What hadn't dawned on me was that i'd also transferred other needs, like those for acceptance, approval and even, let's face it, love, onto your ever-so-reluctant self. I don't think it meant i had any fewer needs of Mom; rather, it increased my overall deficit. It exacerbated all my feelings of your not meeting my needs as a sister, which on their own would have still been way too much for you. Because of this, your power to reduce me to a tongue-tied, inarticulate, unproductive being was huge, and devastating not only to me but to our dynamic. This dynamic had been set up by you speaking to me in a particularly rote, patronizing manner. There are still times when you resort to using that tone of voice, but i've learned not to take it personally any more. In fact, as i read your letter there were moments when i felt you were condescending; you made no acknowledgement of the fact that the reason some of the details were in there was for the edification of other readers and not for me. However, after a few rereadings, and some mulling over it all, i accepted it. I've come to understand that you don't mean to sound that way; it's just how you sometimes cope with feeling awkward or uncomfortable. Happily for me, there are few times these days when i even hear that condescension from you at all.

It has also helped greatly to have you describe your loss in all this. I never could envision you as anything but a super-achiever, so it was impossible for me to have much compassion for you being under pressures that i never understood or experienced. Probably because you and Carl had already taken care of that sort of thing. The flip side of that was that i never allowed myself to cross over into any territory that i felt you or Carl had staked out. I remember saying, "You were the artist, Carl was the brainy one, and i was just the social one." You know, it was kind of ironic to read how i "carried on the tradition you established" in my artwork, because i almost never allowed myself to do any visual art until i left home. I could never have let myself enter your sphere. When i did become an artist, i felt that i was doing it *in spite* of the fact that it was something you also did. I think it had become safe for me because you'd already changed your focus from art to music.

I agree with you that we do have "separate spheres of influence." I've never been one to rise to the challenge of competition; in fact, i kind of wither. But you did neglect to note that i do sing in a wonderful lesbian performing ensemble, and have done so for seven years. While it doesn't provide an income for me, it is a significant part of my life and it bears mentioning. Have i told you that, often, when i sing my solos, i think of you? It inspires me to sing out my best, my strongest (and when i want to concentrate on pitch, i think of Mom). And you know i've told you that i save playing your music for special occasions, because it might be weeks before your voice ceases to resonate in my mind's ear. It's not that i don't enjoy your music; i love it. It's just that it stays with me for so long!

There's so much that's changed between us. This is such a different letter from the one I would have written thirty — or even five — years ago. Even though our basic emotional make-up will always be somewhat polar, i feel that we have more in common all the time. I'm grateful that we are able to hold the love we have for our family between us. I feel that you are finally beginning to value my gifts. By allowing me to contribute to the quality of your life, the power dynamic is at long last more in balance. There's a lot more to say, and i have little doubt we'll say it, so for now i'll end with this. I'm glad we'll be seeing each other again so soon.

I love you.
Julie.

Jan Andrews
and Lynn Andrews

SANDRA WHITWORTH

Left: Lynn   Right: Jan

How We
Know Enough

 Jan

Dear Lynn,

Looking back to when we were kids, I see myself —
long, dark braids flying out behind me, hitting my back
as I run — and you, smaller, more fragile somehow,
racing to catch up.

I'd hang upside down on the bars, my face turning
beet red, and tell you I would die in a few more minutes. Hear you crying to Mom: "Jannie's going to die,
Jannie's going to die …" It felt good knowing you'd
believe me, most times anyway, 'cuz I was older.
We'd fight in the back of our stationwagon — "like
cats and dogs," Mother would say — and we'd both
have teeth marks and scratches to prove it. I'd tell
you that the house would burn down if you kept the
light on in our room all night. You see, your nightmares scared me, too, and maybe you'd stop having
them if I could distract you — or at least I could get
to sleep with the lights off.

I had that physical strength and belief in my body
which means a lot when you're nine or ten, but you
had the strength of your heart's knowledge. I admired
the sheer strength of your convictions, and I still do.

There is something raw and pure in the way you speak of things that matter. You were a fighter: for the crows they wanted to shoot because they made too much noise outside our windows at dawn; for the stuffed animals that we saved from the garbage truck, sneaking out in the cold early morning to collect them from where *he* had dumped them, and bringing them to our friend Jennifer's house; and, later, for yourself and then for me.

As we got older we'd stay up half the night trying to solve the world's problems, but we'd never talk about our own deep secrets until later — much later. There was comfort back then, a protection in not speaking of it — it would make it more real if we did. Through that silent pain, I'd lost my physical self, my body-sense, which was so strong in me as a child.

Then we went travelling out west together as young women, and our trip became another reality I wasn't ready for — you could get hurt and I couldn't stop it, couldn't protect you. Instead I felt guilty; I was the older sister wasn't I? But we were just girls/women in a scary world of men who were bigger and stronger than us. The powerlessness deepened in me. And I came to the full realization of something I had known underneath for a long time — that older didn't necessarily mean wiser or stronger, just older.

Later, for me, there was Rick and a baby — my little "sun," Daniel, who brought me truly alive. You snuck into my hospital room on *your* birthday and took pictures of him when he was brand new, all pink and wrinkled. Sharing in my joy, you made it richer, fuller. I felt a certain pride in the fact that Dan sometimes called you "Mom," too.

Meanwhile, you were going through your own awakening. I don't remember the exact moment when I realized you were with a woman. I think when you wrote me from out west I had already put a few things together. I don't remember feeling shocked, just hurt that another woman could be as close to you as I had been — or even closer. I wondered if I'd be replaced, if you'd go on without me, if you had a different understanding of life now. Could we still share our hearts' secrets with each other? I felt a sadness, a loss, in that moment.

At the same time, I was so happy for you. You always did every-thing with passion and I could feel that your reaching, growing and loving with women was a wonderful coming home to your true self. And, yes, you still gave me your poetry and stayed up and talked with me late into the night; you still wrote me long, wonderful letters about your exciting life; and you were still, always, my sister.

I never had to come out to the family — you did it for me. You've always been a cushion there between the hardness of truth finally spoken and my not wanting to hurt anyone. When I finally had the courage to broach the subject with Mom, she said something like, "I know, dear, as long as you're happy … but what about Dan, how will it affect him?" It was okay for you to be a lesbian — you were always your own person anyway — but I had a family. I'd been with a man in a long-term relationship and had a child. Maybe I was just copying you; maybe it was just a crazy phase that I'd get over.

I believe our family sometimes feels that you and I influence each other too much. Along with this comes the assumption that we will agree on everything and that we — "the kids" — are in some ways interchangeable. It's a quandary for me, because so much of my identity was and is in relation to you — whether I was the same, the opposite or just different. And what I appreciate most about our relationship is that intuitive deep understanding of each other that comes from shared experience, genes, blood, whatever.

There are many similarities in the choices we've made in our lives. Both country girls at heart, we have moved to spacious homes surrounded by pastures and forests. Partners, children, animals — all enrich our lives. (Geographically, the path between our homes now and Ottawa, our growing-up home, form a triangle, each point equidistant from the others.) As lesbian feminists we try to promote a supportive, inclusive and caring society by speaking out about our lives — in the schools, in the community and in our family. I often hear people calling you "Jan" and me "Lynn." It's a good thing we are both secure in our identities, or that could be unsettling! And, in the family, we still play the game of speaking for each other to soften the blow of hard words needing to be said. Yet, I believe we are brave, to live and love as we do.

There are many things that are different about us, too — things I appreciate and acknowledge to be gifts we bring each other. Your creativity and artistic talent have always enriched my life and made me proud. Your ability to make people laugh and come together

with your storytelling is amazing to me. The way you see the
world is much like a child's — with wonder, interest and a desire
to know more about everything. That's probably why you shine
around kids, why they come to you like a magnet. And I am the
solid, logical, down-to-earth plodder who gets things done, and
listens … for your words, for the truth of life in everything. I am
a true Aquarian: justice and compassion are important to me, and,
deep inside, there is a freedom lover who rides her horse across
the open land.

Writing about what you mean in my life is like writing about
life, you know. Who I am has been shaped so much by our growing together — as children and as adults. Even though our lives
are so busy that we don't see as much of each other now, I know
you're always there — like the wise sister-owl you once painted
on a shirt for me, bringing me passion, wisdom and the ability to
see in the night … like the horses in the pasture over there.

Lynn

Lynn

For Jan

Jan

i.

By the mended fence at the real farm of your grown-up life
you explain to me how your horse has amazing peripheral vision
divided by the two halves of her brain.
So with her beautiful doe eyes she may believe
she sees each of us twice every seeing a new experience.
She turns her head sideways in greeting as we approach
a cone of blindness in front
sees everything larger than life startles easily.

I am squinting over her dusty back looking up at you listening
the real horse blowing her soft breath into my ear and the sun suddenly
keen in such perfect relation
and just then in my tunnel vision, you begin to float backwards into
the tiny lawn of the past.

ii.

The scarf with the green horseshoe border
Flicka's chestnut face wrapped around the top of your head
ends knotted under your chin
tall for nine and already sniffing the breeze
cantering around the backyard in your bare feet
jumping
all the obstacles leaping
over mother's broom handles raised and carefully balanced
on the arms of unravelling plastic lawn chairs   bounding
over rickety wooden sawhorses nicking your hooves on lengths of the
striped double skipping rope anchored to the apple tree on one end
me holding the other taut

a little bored
but knowing you are serious
"higher" you shout
anything higher
your long black pony tail flying

iii.

She is   everyone is
older
protector   she is stronger than me
runs faster is bravest   though she rarely speaks
her and her shy turn
stubborn and graceful
in the sun she climbs higher and her shouts filter down through the dry
leaves of the tallest elm tree she is always at the top of
in the fort we all want her to be boss

indoors she folds herself like a kite closing
she is silence
so no one at the dinner table will notice
how strong she is
how she swallows the wind

how she is.

They do not realize
she is Flicka and Black Beauty and Snow Cloud and Blaze.
They think she is just a girl

but I know about the wind
about our mother whose eyes she looks out of

and of course
about how I am different
from her.

iv.

She is stronger than me
or i believe her to be and make it so
she is stronger
in body   doesn't get sick protects me from nightmares and things in
the night that are not real

I   afraid of the Dark
she afraid of what is in the dark

peripheral vision
does she see him arriving twice?

v.

Write about your sister.

Think about your breathing
and you begin to breathe all
out   of
rhythm feel a need for more air.

I am afraid
sister/my self sister
to break the rope   thread
of protection   rare
gossamer
connection
we are everenders on.

vi.

Write about your sister.
Here's one for you. The silken filament of the common orb weaver is a
thousand times stronger than steel of the same thickness
and by far

more elastic

watch it stretch up to double its length
without breaking.

Is a mirror too sacred
too simple?

broke from
and through
the weight of your father's pain
your father

just think about your sister

and feel your self conscious
lungs expanding
beyond silence

vii.

I want to rescue her
am fiercer
but so small
smaller than everyone
inside   I hear voices
speak mostly with animals
am easily distracted
watching the only gift of the poppy in June
revealing so brief a thought

have nightmares
of long division and intersecting lines.

Geometry favours her
numbers are drawn in her hands
she holds up orange and apple planets knowing eventually i will
understand their turning
explains things
so patiently   sees i haven't understood
sees that i exist in some parallel universe
she is calm and determined to make me appreciate
the beauty of logic with its domino light

I am younger
but rooted into the past beyond his reach
a small scaled dragon
fire to her water emotional frequently sick more easily hurt
more easily fixed

I am stronger
than her
I must teach her to fly

viii.

Sister mirror mother
mirror
tiptoe out in the dark of night

all of my sisters

look very closely

it will be hard to breath
then you will see

the Weaver
remaking her web under cover of dark
hanging a single thread between two chosen branches
she will walk
back and forth and back again
adding new strands till thread becomes cable
becomes bridge

see her drop a dragline from the centre point
anchoring
and from the hub begin
to radiate her spokes
attaching each one with a magic disk
her basting threads of pure protein

in silk like secret ink her crosshatch map
mimicking the nectar guides of flower petals

you will see   her
take up her post
on the hub
one leg tuned to her telegraph thread
waiting.

ix.

Write about your mirror   charm
protecting eye of the watcher   the one who knows you
sister
how we know enough

here in our strength   where fear has been
in your eyes in the sun, the horse's face reflected
on the invisible silent map of our childselves with its folds
and tears and hard
marked places

same map
by heart

Write about silence   our lifeblood
family creed like so many boxed lawns of the sixties
my lesbian sister and i who were not then
how we went to war together
comrades, changing the wheel's direction
fought together
twin scars of survival

some hub of sound from where we developed

an ability to produce silk

whispering some words
just out
side of the law
just off of the family map

we sisters
choosing ourselves

said a web of truth

a miracle
to catch a future in

my sisters all

bound by blood and bone and reflection
her turn of phrase, your smallest gesture, my own laughter

go ahead
write about
your beloved sister

Left: Jan
Right: Lynn

TO SAPPHO, MY SISTER

Ursula Steck
and Eva Steck

Left: Ursula   Right: Eva

Enjoying the
Difference

Ursula

Dear Lee Fleming,

I read on euro-sappho [the internet] about your book
on lesbian sisters. I have just arrived back home from
the German lesbian spring meeting in Hamburg. My sister Eva and I were both there and had a great time. Now
that I'm back at work and alone in the office, I thought
I'd take the chance to tell you a little of our story. If you
are interested in including any of it in your book, I
would, of course, have to talk to my sister first.

I am thirty years old and live in Cologne, Germany.
My sister, Eva, is twenty-seven and lives in Göttingen
(close to Kassel). We have no other siblings. Eva has
studied to be a teacher and currently works in an old
mill, selling biological food and agricultural supplies.
She is training to become a therapeutic riding teacher.
She is also active in lesbian project work and is very
politically minded. I work as an editorial assistant for
a law journal. I am also a freelance journalist and am
working on a book of poetry with the working title
"Grenzland" (borderland).

My parents married in 1964, after my mother had
been pregnant with me for three months. In 1974, my

father became a full professor of mechanics at the University of Braunschweig/Niedersachsen and we all moved to a little village only two kilometres from the East German border.

For me, life in the village meant nature, animals (Eva and I both had ponies we took care of and rode each day, although we didn't often do this together) and the ways of the village people, which fascinated me. I was an absolute tomboy, although I never wanted to be a boy — I wanted to be a girl who looked and behaved like a boy. I've been fascinated by androgyny ever since. My childhood friends were daughters of farmers as well as girls from the city, but I never felt that I really belonged. Many people in our village were originally from Eastern Europe and almost everybody had relatives in East Germany. The border and the Second World War were daily topics. The cold war atmosphere was a constant presence in my childhood. The topic of the inter-German border and borderlines has since influenced my thinking and, especially, my creativity. It is ironic that, as an adult, I live in Cologne, which is as far from the former border as you can get in Germany.

After graduating from high school, I lived for a year on a huge farm one hundred kilometres from my parents' place, where I worked in the household and garden and with the animals. Already I had begun to develop symptoms, which today are quite prominent, of my disease of the muscles. It became clear that I couldn't continue to work in a profession that required hard physical work. So, in 1984, I decided to move to Cologne and study. I went to Canada a couple of times and began to specialize in Canadian women's literature. In 1991, I graduated from university and began to work at the Institute of Air and Space Law. For the first two years I was still working on a PhD thesis, but my interest in creative writing took over more and more, and I now make my living by writing and editing.

For almost nine years, I lived with three other people — one woman and two men (all straight) — in a flat in the center of Cologne and I just recently moved into a new flat with an old friend of mine, Andrea, who is also straight. One of the big differences between Eva and me is that she has decided to live her life mostly and quite exclusively with lesbian friends and in the lesbian community, while I have many straight friends — male and female — in addition to my gay and lesbian friends. We have talked about this sometimes, but not too intensely. Somehow I have the feeling that it has mostly to do with the different cities in which we live. Cologne is very mixed in every sense. We have one of the largest lesbian and gay populations in Europe. To live as a lesbian in Cologne has become quite an unspectacular thing in the last few years (at least in my experience).

Göttingen, where Eva lives, is a small city with a huge University. The whole atmosphere of the city is aggressive because of the confrontation between the political spirit of many of the students and the conservative mindset of the majority of the non-student population. Every political demonstration in Göttingen can lead to a breakdown of "normal" everyday life, just because of the relatively small size of the town and the hysterical reaction of the police. In Göttingen, it's difficult to be out as a lesbian and safe from harassment. Many of the women cling together strongly and form closed groups. Cologne's mix of people with different lifestyles, ethnic backgrounds and sexual orientations would be almost impossible to realize in Göttingen.

I have a disability I inherited from our mother (fortunately, Eva did not inherit it). It's a disease of the muscles which makes my body movements quite different from other people's and challenges me in many everyday situations. It's funny: Although Eva and I live quite far away from each other and only meet a couple of times each year, and although most of my difficulties developed after I moved away from my parents' house thirteen years ago, Eva is an accomplished helper. She is physically very strong but is also extremely sensitive — a great combination.

Lee, after this long narration (I initially only wanted to send you a short message and ask for more information on your project), I am looking forward to hearing from you. Good luck already with your book.

blue skies
ursula

Left: Eva   Right: Ursula

Dear Lee,

I was delighted to read your e-mail this morning, especially because I spoke to Eva yesterday evening on the phone, and told her about your project, and she loved it. She told me that she has wished for a long time to meet or learn about other lesbian sisters. I promised her to ring her as soon as I had notice from you and so I will do that tonight. I will also send her all the information you gave me about the book. She is not connected to e-mail but I'm sure with a combination of snail mail and e-mail, communication amongst the three of us will be fine. Now, I would like to add further details to the story I have already sent you.

Our coming out to each other is a funny story. As children we were not overly fond of each other and had a lot of fights. Our relationship started (very slowly) to become better after I turned eighteen and left home, but for many years we were still quite suspicious of each other. I had the feeling that we just could not accept each other's differences. Both of us had relationships with men; Eva's were long, mine only brief. We both developed a big interest in feminism, but neither of us knew that the other one shared this interest. I had always fallen in love with women (I don't know about Eva in this respect) but had seldom allowed this fact to enter my conscious mind. If I did think about it (especially in my early twenties) I smiled about it and found it interesting and daring, but never even considered that I might be lesbian. In fact, only a few weeks before Eva came out to me I had very consciously been physically attracted to a woman I had just met, but I still refused to consider that I was lesbian.

Three years ago (when we were still distant in our relationship with each other, although warmer than we had been in childhood) Eva rang me. She was at a women's congress in Bonn, close to Cologne. (This was when I realized that she was interested in feminism.) She wanted to meet and have dinner with me. On the phone, she sounded like it was important and I wondered why, especially since she and our mother were planning to visit me two weeks later. In any case, I agreed to meet Eva in Bonn and we had supper at an Italian restaurant. I asked her how the conference was, and if there were any lesbian working groups (even then, it never entered my mind that she could be lesbian herself). She told me about the conference, and after dinner she told me that she knew for certain that she was lesbian.

I remember feeling the same way I had when friends had come out to me. I was momentarily very shocked — especially that I could have been so blind — and then extremely joyful and pleased. I expressed this to Eva and we talked about her being a lesbian. I told her I thought it was great that she had discovered herself in this way; I also told her that I thought I was straight because I had never fallen in love with a woman. After dinner, we decided to go to the women's café in Bonn, and Eva said that judging by my style of dressing and haircut, I could be a lesbian. I just remember feeling pleased by this ...

Well, two weeks later I fell in love with a woman consciously and wonderfully, and I felt that I had finally arrived at my true identity and could feel happy. (This has so far proved to be absolutely true.) I rang Eva and only told her that I had met this woman and that I was in love. She wanted to know all about the woman I was in love with and never even commented on the fact of my coming out. I loved this reaction.

I confess that, when it first became clear to me that both Eva and I were lesbians, I was anxious about whether Eva would take me seriously and accept me. As the older one, I was used to the childhood dynamic where Eva was "doing what I was doing." When she developed interests similar to mine, I wouldn't take her seriously in the beginning. I would think that she was copying me. Sometimes it was even hard for Eva herself to distinguish her true interests from interests that copied mine. And, because there were only the two of us, we were constantly compared, even though we looked and behaved very differently. The points of comparison were mostly interests and passions.

Now, Eva was the first: the first to come out, the first to admit an "interest" (her love for women) which determined her whole life. And there I was, three weeks later, calling to tell her: "Well, by the way, I think I have a real crush on somebody, her name is ... " I was both excited and a little bit anxious about her reaction. Anyway, her reaction was wonderful because it was so calm and relaxed. And suddenly everything changed: Before, we had always been cautious with each other because we were (or at least I thought we were) so different; now, we were linked on a level far deeper than the level of our differences.

Lee, so much for a "brief" account! I guess I just love writing too much. Maybe what I have written so far sounds too matter of fact, not subjective enough …? More will follow next week. First, I have to survive Christopher Street Day (Gay Pride) on the weekend. I'm in the parade and already dying of excitement.

Have a great day,
ursula

Dear Lee,

Eva has called me today, but unfortunately I only received her message via my answering machine. She is finally back from her holiday and said that she was in the process of writing. We will meet soon to talk, work and take pictures. After that, I will be able to send you her text.

I'd like to add a few (don't worry — really only a few) paragraphs to what I've already written. They will deal with ambivalent emotions and I'll try to describe our family and the way my ideas about life and the future have developed and changed.

I think my and Eva's differences are positive features. I believe it is our big differences that prevent us from having feelings of rivalry. We live far from each other and have very different lifestyles. I do not want to compare myself to Eva. She is very active doing the things she loves: sports, making political commitments, having her own women/lesbian friends and groups. I am active with writing, network activism, Buddhism, my women/lesbian/het/gay friends. Eva and I share a love of music and books, and we exchange discoveries, especially about women's writing or women's music. I like the way she looks and styles herself, and I (most of the time) like my own body and looks. I enjoy the fact that we do not resemble each other very much. I find it fascinating that our parents could produce daughters with such different features.

Eva and I have become close and trusting friends, and despite our very different personalities and lifestyles, we respect each other deeply. I have told our mother that I am in love with a woman and her reaction has been very relaxed. I have the feeling that she would have reacted in the same way if I had told her I was in a heterosexual relationship. (Our mother was never that interested in our love life, mostly, we guess, because she did not really want us to marry and live with men. She is happy that we can develop lives where we can discover who we are and do the things we love without anybody — for mother, this means any husband — hindering us.) Eva, who is even closer to our mother than I, has never spoken to her about lesbian love, but we believe she knows about Eva being a lesbian anyhow. Neither Eva nor I have talked to our father about this topic. Eva's relationship to him is not very close. They just don't seem to speak the same language and often hurt each other. As for myself, I have decided to come out to him only after I have been in a relationship for a longer period of time. Our father has the sort of mind where he believes something and takes it seriously only when he can see the evidence. So far, contact with my parents has not been a big factor in my relationships, as my parents live more than five hours by car from Cologne and I only visit them once or twice a year.

I was always glad that the disease of the muscles which I inherited from our mother was not passed on to Eva. The reasons for this are complex, I guess. On a selfish level, I have to admit that it is sometimes difficult to see a mirror image of your own movements and gestures. When these movements are far from the norm, prominent and often problematic, it does not make things easier. Sometimes, for example, I find it strange to be with my mother. Her body is very different from my own, but when she makes sudden movements that I recognize as peculiar to my own body, I experience a feeling of alienation. This is often painful, especially when my psyche also transmits guilt for having such emotions. When Eva and I are together, life is much easier in this respect. On a more compassionate level, I am happy that Eva does not have to face the practical and emotional problems that come with this disease. (Although I know that this might be too easy a view. I am quite sure that she has to face her own processes connected with my physical situation.) On a purely practical level, it is great to be with Eva because it feels like we can go anywhere we want to go. She is so strong that I know she could just carry me, if necessary. And she is very natural in the way she approaches this situation.

Rivalry? Hmmmm. Somehow it feels a bit strange to write only positive things about my relationship with my sister. But I am very enthusiastic about us — especially because our relationship has improved so much in the last few years and today I feel extremely good about it. Anyhow, there has been rivalry before and maybe we will have to face it again one day. I hope it won't be over lovers, although I am quite optimistic about that. So far, my own internal boundaries have always worked very well when a woman I like is with somebody else, and I have never fallen in love with the lover of a close friend (or of my sister). I have an intuition that Eva's built-in boundaries are similar. More dangerous is the issue of "best friends." As a child, I sometimes interefered in Eva's friendships; I was older and more talkative and therefore in the stronger position. I know that the things that happened then have created wounds which can still hurt Eva today in similar situations. I sincerely hope I have learned my lesson.

For me, being lesbian means not only having a sexual orientation towards women, it means "to love women." This doesn't mean that I love every woman I meet, of course, but that I am oriented as a woman towards women. To be a feminist (which I was long before I discovered I was lesbian) is to love the beauty of women, to be loyal to women, to forge strong bonds with women, to feel for the women of the world, to LIVE with women. And this is now something that Eva and I share. This outlook on life connects us more strongly than any biological link had connected us before.

I had always thought that my relationship with my sister was something special, in spite of our differences and lack of closeness. When I left home, I became more grateful to have Eva as a sister — indeed, to have a sister at all. I was glad I wasn't an only child, and I was glad that I had a sibling with whom communication was possible. But Eva, my sister, as a friend? I felt that the links between us were too compulsory and not free enough for friendship. Now, it is through our love for women — something each of us discovered and developed on her own — that we have a strong mutual tie outside of our compulsory ties. When combined with our sisterhood, this bond seems indestructible.

blue skies
ursula

Eva

I fell in love with a girl for the first time when I was fourteen. My first sexual experience with another woman occurred when I was twenty-one, but, after that, it took me another four years to come out as a lesbian to myself, my friends and some of my family. The first member of my family I told about my lesbian identity was my sister Ursula.

I can remember the evening very well. I had been attending a feminist congress in Bonn, a city near where Ursula lives. She picked me up and we went to a restaurant together. We had a lovely evening there, laughing and talking. When I finally mustered my courage and told her that I was a lesbian, she wasn't even surprised. Two weeks later, she called me to tell me that she had fallen in love with a woman herself.

Since that phone call, my relationship with Ursula, which had been rather distant, has become closer and closer and more intense. Today, my sister is one of my best friends.

Ursula and I live about 400 kilometres apart from each other. Cologne, where Ursula lives, is a multicultural metropolis, while my town, Göttingen, is a provincial university town. Because of our distance from each other, our very different personalities and Ursula's disability, we lead very different lives. But, in spite of this, we take part in each other's everyday lives. We talk to each other on the phone regularly, and discuss relationships, family and everything we have done or experienced that might be of interest. We exchange useful information, which mostly means that Ursula roots up information and addresses I can use in projects I'm working on, such as planning and organizing a congress for lesbians in this region or producing a women's/lesbian calendar.

Somehow Ursula knows more people and hears about more things than I do. I think this is partly a result of our different personalities — she is more outgoing and open to other people than I am. It is also a result of our different lifestyles — Ursula lives in a city and is connected to computer networks and mailboxes that reach other women and lesbians all over the country, Europe and North America. I do not use computers at all and tend to work and socialize with a small and closely knit group of women. As well, Ursula does not work in far-left lesbian/feminist politics like I do.

Fortunately, our differences don't separate us or create problems. In fact, they are complementary. It is interesting for each of us to hear about, and take part in, the other one's very different life. I find it helpful to get advice from somebody who knows me very well but has some distance from my life and the people in it.

Though the telephone is the "lifeline" of our friendship, it is not our only way of connecting with each other. This spring, we both attended the German lesbian congress in Hamburg and met with each other and some friends. We also visit each other and have met some of each other's closer friends. One of my best friends is now a friend of Ursula's as well, and we have visited her together twice.

All of my good friends know a lot about Ursula and how important she is to me. Though we don't see each other often, she has an important role in my everyday life.

Why am I glad that both my sister and I are lesbians? After I came out, I found that being a lesbian shaped my consciousness and lifestyle significantly. As a consequence, I found it increasingly difficult to maintain relationships with my heterosexual women friends. The gap between us grew wider and wider; I became more and more separatist and woman-identified. For the most part, I now

Left: Ursula   Right: Eva

lead a lesbian-only lifestyle. Apart from my work, where I do meet men and heterosexual women, I'm surrounded by other lesbians.

I don't consider lesbians to be my friends automatically, but I find that if women have sympathies for each other, they can have a very strong bond. Being a lesbian means that you have a lot of experiences you can only share with other lesbian women — experiences to do with coming out, relationships, sex, discrimination, problems with family ... I am quite a political person, and this means that my analysis of society and my goals are defined by my lesbian/feminist point of view.

The fact that my sister is a lesbian means that we not only share our past, but also our present. We share the knowledge of what it was like to grow up in our family *and* we share the knowledge of what it is like to live as lesbian women in Germany in the 1990s. We share an outlook on life.

I don't know if lesbian sisters are always very close to each other, but Ursula and I certainly are. We are not necessarily closer than very good friends but our closeness feels different to me. Maybe this is because I have absolute trust in her — a trust which comes from knowing her all my life.

Left: Eva   Right: Ursula

Gillean Chase
and Janet Bianic

Left: Gillean   Right: Janet

DEVON SIERRA

Strangers,
Sisters

Gillean and Janet

Janet:

The kerosene lamp demands little. I light it, squeeze lime into my Corona beer. The silence inside the cabin and the light of the lamp remind me of the country farm where I grew up.

Gillean:

How does one write about a stranger to whom one is related? We grew up in Alberta on a 160 acre farm. Our parents produced wheat and oats, poultry, beef and ten children. I was the oldest of six at home, with older brothers and a sister grown and gone.

When Janet and I were children, our three years' difference in age meant a great deal. Janet was in elementary school when I was in junior high, in Grade Nine when I was in Grade Twelve. I graduated from university with a degree in education and began my career as a high-school English teacher for a Catholic school board, not because of my religious preferences but because they offered me a teaching position. I was technically Roman Catholic — exposed to catechism, if not to church — and expected to teach religion to seniors along with my English literature courses. My department head was a nun in full habit, and monks navigated the corridors; so did a woman with whom I fell deeply in love.

My free time was curtailed by marking and preparing lessons. Any social time I had was spent wooing this woman whom I did not have the courage to do more with than kiss. I learned to write impassioned, if obscure, poetry and a very literary (read: "unpublishable") novel, being afraid to voice the love that dared not speak its name. We agonized about our mutual feelings for each other until she took the summer off to travel to Hawaii. When she came back, she married a teacher on staff. Catholic guilt was too much for both of us.

Meanwhile, Janet had finished high school and began her life as a working adult. Neither of us spoke much to the other. Every once in a while, we would drive the miles it took to visit our parents, share food and not very much else about our personal lives.

When I was twenty-five, I joined a consciousness-raising group, discovered feminism and changed my name, and had the courage to make love with a woman. In a burst of spiritual fervour, I came out to my family over dinner. After dropping these bombs, I went blithely off, leaving them to wonder how I could want to be a Jew, and why I didn't like the name I had been given. My lesbianism apparently wasn't part of the ensuing conversation.

Janet:

I am hynotized by the rain and the memory of the kerosene lamp. I will celebrate winter solstice with my sister tomorrow night in Vancouver. What part of me will I share, what part will remain sacred, protected from the light? I am a story, accompanied by black and white photographs taken inside my father's house: black or white; either/or; "my way or there's the door."

I had learned so well to contain my opinions at the dinner table and to observe the emotional exchanges of others that, when my sister announced, "I've changed my name to Gillean Chase, the name I'll use when I'm published. I've converted to Judaism and I'm a lesbian," I merely adjusted my glasses and peered up at the conversation unravelling before my eyes. I think Mom said something about having chosen Gillean's name, but this was drowned out by my father's comment: "We are Catholics. Even your mother changed her religion to be Catholic."

TO SAPPHO, MY SISTER

It was about then that I stood up and began the dishes. Holy shit, I thought, what part of this are we addressing? The dishes became more friendly and familiar than anything else I could find to hang on to.

How many times had I already made love to Dawn? I had not once considered that I, too, was a lesbian. I was accepted by Dawn's family as her best friend, another place-setting at the family's Sunday dinner. I shopped at her uncle's corner store, drank cherry Coke and rye with her cousins, assembled jigsaw puzzles with them on many Christmas eves. I watched her postman father darn woollen socks and laughed at his corny jokes. How could I be a lesbian? How could I fit into a labelled box? When I checked back in to our family dinner, all I could hear was me.

Gillean:

A few times, Janet brought her friend Dawn home. Our creepy brother Gene would try to get Dawn alone so he could put the moves on her, as he had on me when I was a child. I didn't know this at the time, but Gene had also assaulted Janet. All I knew was that I wasn't going to leave Dawn alone so that Gene could manipulate her into bed. So I'd stoically sit beside Dawn whenever Gene tried to lure her upstairs, away from family members.

During this process, I developed quite a crush on Dawn. I wordlessly mooned over her and occasionally held hands with her on the couch. I read her tea leaves and tried to see myself in her romantic future. Eventually, Dawn fell head over heels in love with a Jamaican man and married him.

Meanwhile, Janet had become a corporate success in her job with an oil company. She had the charm necessary for a public-relations job and the ability to deal with business concerns and international tycoons.

Janet:

I moved to a northern community in midwinter 1974, not only to accept a job opportunity with an oil company but to begin a relationship with a man. I lived with him for fourteen years. Lawren was a calming anchor who often said, "Whatever you think is right, dear." Even if those words were not true, I needed to believe in his respect for my point of view. But his stillness, his reserve and his passivity left me very empty.

I took comfort in my professional accomplishments and it was through my career that I met a married woman who caused my lips to tingle, and my spirit to plummet when I did not see her. We both had expense accounts, which allowed us to meet in various hotel rooms and taste Châteauneuf-du-Pape, rack of lamb — and each other's lips. This relationship ended when Lawren and I built our new house — still unwed and uncommitted.

Then, at a surprise party for my thirty-fifth birthday, a friend choreographed the beginnings of our wedding by choosing a date for us to be married. Planning the wedding was simple, but the actual ceremony was quite another story. Having no idea of our mutual reluctance, friends rallied around the "event of the year," bursting with excitement. Dad had passed away a decade earlier, so I chose my youngest brother to be the one who would walk me along the red carpet in the open garden near our home. On my last morning as a single woman, I watched my friends' preparations. I did not know that, five years later, I would leave Lawren to become a lesbian.

In late 1989, I joined my sister Gillean for dinner at a restaurant and was introduced to her long-term lover. Then my female lover outed me over the oysters: "I'm not her first," she said. "And what do you mean you didn't know Jan is a lesbian?" Gillean was giggly and full of questions; and I was relieved, at some level, that the issue was on the table. Gillean's partner shrugged when I caught her eye. "Hey. Don't look at me," she said. "I'm just having dinner."

Gillean:

I didn't know my sister was a lesbian until I was forty, when I was faced with the realization that I had a sister with a twenty-year history of involvement in lesbian relationships about which I knew nothing. In fact, I had supposed that telling Janet about my lesbianism had resulted in her rejection of me. For example, when she married Lawren, I was not invited to her reception, even though my brother was invited. I sent her a sarcastic card of congratulation, indicating that perhaps I would be invited to her next wedding. Sheepishly, she responded that she didn't think I had any use for weddings and she didn't want to rub my nose in one.

Janet:

After breaking up with Lawren, I had relocated to Vancouver and absorbed myself in self-development workshops, searching for the threads of my spirituality. I was in the right city for exploring. I found peace in Native beliefs and culture, and I even made and painted a few drums, one of which delighted Gillean on her birthday. I spent a wonderful four years believing I was in the right place at the right time, designing courses and grounding myself by observing other people's skills and behaviour.

Gillean:

Janet and I saw more of each other after she moved to Vancouver, although our visits were still periodic and fit into busy lives built around different priorities. I went through having breast cancer and wrote my first published novel. My lover, Leslie, developed lung cancer and a giant sense of grievance at the world in general, and Janet in particular. She resented working at a meaningless government job while Janet took New Age workshops and marketed her skills in community development.

Janet:

Gillean didn't tell me about having breast cancer until we discussed it in the context of Leslie's chemotherapy. Meanwhile, I was in shock until Leslie came out of the hospital. Remembering the skin cancer that had eaten our mother, I sure couldn't be there emotionally for Leslie, amidst the smells and sounds of a hospital so like the one in which our mother had died. And Gillean had done it to me again: she had made a major announcement about life-threatening illnesses in the same way she had casually proclaimed her name change, sexuality and religion.

Gillean:

Leslie became unusually silent and uncommunicative. I sensed that she resented Janet for being "privileged" — a woman who had financial assets at a time when Leslie was struggling to keep her small cabin on the Gulf Islands. Leslie couldn't afford New Age workshops; not for us the pleasure of going to Starhawk's witch camp or on vacations to the Southwest, where we wanted so deeply to go.

Janet might say that doing what you want is about making choices, but I, too, had some resentment about the work she did in order to be able to make these choices — ruining the environment of the North and exploiting Natives. However, I could also see Janet growing into a staunch environmentalist and caretaker of the earth; I saw her Native spirit coming out of hiding as she accepted responsibility for her daily habits of consumption and chose to use products that would conserve the environment. When she hand-painted my drum, full of magical images and pulsing with the voice of the stick, I drummed with joy for the love I had regained for my young sister.

Janet:

On Hallow's Eve, a few years ago, I brought two eight-pound pumpkins and a new lover to Gillean and Leslie's traditional pumpkin carving, which we always celebrated with sacred words and rituals. This proved too much for my young friend, who accused them of "devil worship" and left me to carve alone. I was embarrassed, and secretly desired a partner who liked ritual.

Those who ask, receive. I soon met Andrea, a red-headed Leo with the energy of a whirlwind. It became common for us to speak three hours a day on the telephone, and for me to take days to sort through the content of each conversation, never quite catching up with "myself," with my emotional responses and my role in this relationship. I was intrigued, and hoped that one day I would learn to be as emotional as Andrea, and less intellectualizing and cautious.

Gillean:

Meeting Andrea was a bit like taking a roller-coaster ride. She was warmth and fire, vulnerability and innocence. She called herself a shaman and Leslie, who had wanted a spiritual teacher, offered Andrea a crystal healing, which included balancing Andrea's chakras in the bedroom while Andrea lay naked. I fought down a curious uneasiness — not being the jealous kind — and believed Andrea's avowals that she was deeply in love with my sister and that there would never be another woman in her life. This was it for her — a marriage of souls. She loved Janet's independence and her careful emotional approach to things. In this balance of opposites, I watched Janet give in to Andrea's coaxing and do something that had been so difficult for her: make a life commitment to being with a woman. This choice was not made easier for Janet by the fact that Andrea was a survivor of Satanic ritual abuse.

Janet:

How can I describe the hazards of becoming involved with a woman who sees open flirtation as non-threatening, who defines monogamy as being able to do everything with another woman except make love? And what is making love? Is it long intimate walks, feeding the ducks, naked crystal healings, expensive gifts — pouring all the wine into the glass of someone else's partner?

I'm not quite sure how to describe the feelings of betrayal I started to experience when my lover, Andrea, began to phone Leslie three times a day. How do I describe the feeling of sinking in quicksand that comes from observing incongruent behaviour and actions? Who would want to have a conversation about seduction with a seducer? Who would choose to warm themselves beside a snake in the grass?

Gillean:

Andrea and Leslie spent hours together, playing, shopping, going for intimate lunches and giving each other five-minute hugs upon greeting and parting. Leslie freely admitted being sexually attracted to Andrea — and I sure wasn't getting five-minute hugs or flowers. It bothered me that Leslie gave Andrea the same Hathor necklace that she had given me for one of our anniversaries, and that she phoned Andrea from a limousine as we celebrated our last sad Valentine's Day together. Meanwhile, Andrea was thanking me for being so accepting of her love for Leslie, and crying that Janet just didn't understand their true and non-sexual friendship.

Janet:

I suppose what I contributed to all this was the delivery of my lover to the enemy, on the one hand; and, on the other hand, the opportunity to reconnect with my sister and with our blood relationship. I asked her to hold the phone while I cried into it. In our mutual vulnerability, I saw us as warriors, capable of taking ourselves into the future and of laying the past to rest. Leslie had confessed that she thought Gillean would take her own life if ever she left her. This troubled me for the first three months after their break-up. It comforts me that Gillean's choice to stay in their familiar apartment works for her. It is a reminder of our separateness and our responsibility to ourselves.

Gillean:

It was touch-and-go at first. I felt so much anger toward Leslie, and a sense of Andrea's obliviousness, her tendency not to see me or validate my choices as a person. But how right it is to part when the loving is done, to let the deadwood go and make room for the excitement of being desirable to someone else. In the ashes of ending, I found Carol, and rediscovered my passion and romanticism. She is the gift I never expected — my friend and companion. I wish for Janet the strength of another love, and a sense of wonder about her unique contributions to the world and to our relationship. Her perceptions and choices give me so much to contemplate and learn as we grow toward the fifth decade of our lives on this planet; sisters who are no longer strangers.

Left: Janet   Right: Gillean

Anne-Marie Pedler
and Robyn Pedler

Left: Robyn   Right: Anne-Marie

Sisters-in-Print

Anne-Marie

My sister Robyn and I are often mistaken for each other. At public wimmin's events, wimmin will greet me enthusiastically and launch into a conversation that appears to pick up on a previous one. These conversations can be of an intimate, private nature, or just general and familiar. At times, I've found myself in the middle of tricky situations, where I'm being trusted with something that is meant for Robyn. If I can get in early enough, I tell them that I'm Anne-Marie, "the other one!" Robyn says the same thing often happens to her.

"The other one" is a phrase that we started to use as children, in response to grown-ups who mixed us up in the crowd of our Pedler and McCracken cousins. We lived in a small, rural district in lower Eyre Peninsula, in South Australia. My three sisters and I were referred to as "the girls," whereas our brother had his own name. I am the second of five of my mother's children. There's an older girl, Veronica (now forty-seven), me (forty), Robyn (thirty-eight), Denis (thirty-six) and Therese (thirty-two). My mother, Nita, died in 1962 at age thirty-seven, giving birth to twins. Only one twin, Therese, survived.

My mother had seven sisters and a brother, all but three of whom lived and raised their kids in the same district. These women were called "The McCracken Sisters" even after they married and lost their names. We had about twenty McCracken cousins and were often called "Nita McCracken's girls."

We were also called "Bob Pedler's girls." Dad had four brothers and six sisters. All of his brothers and two of his sisters had families in and around our township, Cummins. We had fifty-seven first cousins on Dad's side, and most of them were surnamed "Pedler." We all went to the same local country Area School, and it was standard procedure to answer the teacher's question "Which Pedler are you?" by replying, "Bob Pedler's," and then, "The second one: Anne-Marie." Even if we hadn't given our surname, the trouble was the Pedlers all looked alike. You didn't have to say anything or give a name; you just had to show your face and you were identified as one of the Pedlers.

The same thing occurred with the McCrackens. There weren't many people in the district who bore the McCracken name, but there was a McCracken "quality." The McCracken wimmin all had high profiles as good organizers, good housekeepers, smart dressers, savvy money-stretchers, hard workers. They were good rural women who excelled at most things. Mum spent a lot of time with her sisters, so we saw ourselves — and were seen by most of the community — as being one of the McCracken women's productions. Physically, the McCrackens were marked, too: The McCracken "look" included big bosoms, big curvy bottoms and a certain assured bearing.

Early on, I took it for granted that I'd be named, known and seen by my tribe and its subsets. We were Pedlers: Bob and Nita's; we were attached to the McCrackens; and I was one of "the girls." Boys keep all their names, so after our brother Denis came along, we were called his as well: "Denis and the girls." My particular name, Anne-Marie, was a detail that would be given up to those who made it through to the intimate inner circle. I was accustomed to being characterized affectionately, to being known and named in relation to community. Unfortunately, though, there were presumptions made about you personally, based on the known characteristics of the Pedlers or the McCrackens: sporty, funny, larrikinish, sociable, musical, smart ... and straight.

Some of this is useful for naming my life as a lesbian. I know there's a tribe of us and that we're each distinct within it. I know that lesbians are often regarded as being alike, as if we look alike and all come from the same prototype (manhaters or vinegar-tits or stunted unnatural women). I also know that some lesbians are happier being with "the girls" and their sisters, and that others prefer to take after "the father's side" and to hang out with the boys.

Having a sister who's a dyke (as well as having at least seven dyke cousins) has given me a benchmark for my perception of reality, and it is one that resists the lies given us about lesbians. Like most lies, they succeed because they are huge ones rather than small ones. They are lies like: lesbians are rare, not common; lesbians are invented by some aberrant action of our own — an individual or solitary pathological whimsy; and lesbians are unconnected to family or other mainstream realities. Having a sister who shares the same mother, who shares the landscape of my childhood, who has her own distinct stories about our shared reality, gives me my benchmark. It says that, as a lesbian, I'm merely one among many; it says that I, as a lesbian, am a story derived from within my family and their stories. It says that my lesbianism is part of the whole story and that, when lesbianism is left out of anything, the story is either incomplete or a lie.

Part of my story goes like this: Nita died giving birth to Therese when I was eight and Robyn was six. It happened in November 1962 — a few days after my birthday, and one day before Robyn's. Three Sagittarians and two lesbians out of five kids: Nita would have been pleased, I think. With her death, we became dramatically distinguished from all the other Pedlers: We were "poor Nita's children." Of "poor Nita's" five children, Veronica and Denis remained living on the farm; the baby Therese was fostered by Nita's sister in Port Lincoln, thirty miles from home; and Robyn and I were the "two girls sent to the nuns" who ran a boarding school in Port Lincoln.

From 1963 to 1970, I lived — with Robyn and twenty or so other boarders — in a kind of extended-family situation, under the nuns' care. These nuns ran the Port Lincoln Catholic school. They were a group of five women of the Josephite Sisters' Order, whose particular mission was to serve the rural poor in Australia. From them, I had great models for women living together, joined in common purpose and order of life, and practising common rule — women who made eye contact with each other, who occupied positions of authority, and who possessed competence and a passion for things and causes. The pity of it, of course, was that their connection with women's culture and women's community was covert, and it was only permitted subsequent to an overt primary affiliation to god, the father, the son. These days I see the same deal going on with "het" women (who work to improve men, not women) or mothers of sons (who present an image of motherhood like that of the Queen Mother to the Son, from whom they inherit "normality" and privilege) or the gayette sisters (who present lesbians as the "other half" of the man thing): they do insist on doing good works for the boys as a kind of ransom paid for the chance to be among women.

I stayed at the boarding school for eight years, and Robyn stayed for ten years. When we were children, Robyn was smaller than me, had milk-white hair and resembled my cousin Marie. I had brown hair, looked like Dad (everyone said so) and was the first one in the family to get surgical stitches — five on one foot. We both played lots of sports and, when she was thirteen, Robyn was tennis captain. This meant that we had to play against each other, and she beat me. She grew taller than me, too. We got into the same amount of trouble at school, but her crimes were things like setting fire to the nuns' shed or sitting in the cook's car without permission or being caught trying to throw out the awful food. My offences were disobedience, talking too much, smoking and making up and reporting exotic "facts" about nuns. I used to tell stories about the nuns to the day-scholars in exchange for food from their homes.

During my fifth year, when I was thirteen, I fell in love with my very best friend Heather. It was a heady time of puberty, love and sex, and kissing behind the locker doors — and Robyn caught us at it. I was a bit worried that she'd tell on us because kissing was against the rules; but I didn't think that Robyn would think kissing was odd — it was just illegal. An important point, but I took it as a given that we both knew to be true, not something to be grateful to Robyn about. At some level, I understood that this lesbian love was normal and part of a real and independent culture, and that it was valid as a result of community and not because an individual person — Robyn or anyone else — permitted or understood or accepted it.

When I was fifteen or so, I experienced internal doubt that went something like this: What if my feeling of "coming home" with women wasn't anything to do with me being myself, an intelligence with a free will? What if it was only the result of some psychiatric equation, like "young plus motherless plus nuns equals aberrant"? For years, though, any theories I wrestled with were always disproved by my looking at Robyn — after all, she had the same life plot and she wasn't weird!

Then we came out to each other. In October 1980, Robyn was twenty-three and I was twenty-five. She was a qualified nurse and had been living in England for a couple of years, while I had been doing the twelve-month European-United Kingdom tour that Australians do. I'd lived with Robyn off and on during that time and was impressed by how competent she was at the business of living in London. During my ten months there, we shared lots of things: the flat, travels, the complexities of the British Rail system, the first London Women's Film Week. She was an interesting person and there was lots to chat about, but I didn't tell her that I'd fallen in love three months before I had left Australia. I didn't read her the letters from Liz, whom she knew slightly; nor did I say how heartsick and homesick I was. I came up with a lame reason for changing my ticket and going home early, before the mandatory twelve months was up (another Australian thing: the tenure for the overseas trips must be twelve months).

In Heathrow Airport, waiting for my plane back to Australia, I casually tried to tell Robyn that best-friendships with wimmin could actually be more than that, and that she might like to consider it as a possibility. I thought I could bolt for the plane if this conversation got too difficult. My attempts to be oblique and not scare her off the idea were wasted; Robyn looked me in the eye, joined all the dots and, what's more, told me *what* this thing was called, *whom* I was in love with, whom *she* was in love with. We had a few minutes to gasp, and then it was time to dash for the plane. We still can't agree who came out first because of the technicalities of implicit and direct speech — and, even if we could sort it out, it would amount to a difference of seconds. She was the second person I'd "come home" to about being a lesbian; after this, I told lots of people within a short period of time.

It is difficult for me to talk about my differences from, and similarities to, my lesbian sister. Any list would be an accumulation of clichés; the trouble, generally, with being a girl in this world is that we're just "those girls in the back of the room" to the "het-pat" eye. We all look alike to them, and the slightest difference can be exaggerated to help the viewer distinguish one from the other. When we were kids, my colour was blue or green and Robyn's was red or pink. I was bookish, she was active; I was serious, she was a wag; I was older, she was younger. On the other hand, we were both called "one of the girls" who were into music and sports, had a gang of friends and were Bob's girls at the convent. Our lives continued to follow the same storyline until we left boarding school and Robyn went to nursing school while I went to teachers' training college. Still, our job choices resembled each other in that we both took "girls' jobs" that didn't require riches to acquire (the state government provided the training and the jobs) so that Dad could reserve his own money for the boy.

Robyn and I are often seen as the same person and as "just one of the girls." And yet, as an adult, I have mostly had a different group of friends and different interests and different work from Robyn's. It's only been in the last eight years that we've lived in the same town. Any lesbian can get lost in that thinking which states: They all look alike to me. Either way — whether through exaggerated differences or bland sameness — the result is a woman diminished. For an endangered species like lesbians, it makes sense that we resemble one another. Camouflage assists survival. Having a sister provides the opportunity to disappear while still being present or represented in the crowd. Having a lesbian sister does the same thing, with a different crowd.

Knowing that Robyn was part of my story in childhood and is part of it now confirms that our lifeline is continuous, that lesbians and lesbianism can be extrapolated from the life of childhood. Lots of lesbians come into their lesbian life at the expense of their previous family life, friends, work. Their family can assume ownership of their childhood, as a way of holding the lesbian ransom. They can say: "If you want a full life, if you want to be reflected by us as the child we knew, then pay us this. We own a piece of you." Lesbianism comes from, and is a part of, my childhood. The "family" doesn't own my childhood; I own it, so I don't pay ransom for it. My sense of ownership may have been less if I hadn't had a lesbian sibling who eventually became part of my lesbian community.

Up until eight years ago, my lovers and friends were, for the most part, separate from Robyn's. I knew her lovers — not very well, but enough to get along with them. I had monogamous relationships that lasted for about four years, and so Robyn got to meet my lovers over a reasonable period of time. She, too, got along with them and, more important, with my group of friends. When she came to live in Adelaide in 1987, I spent more time with her and also got to know her new partner.

A few years later, in 1990 and 1991, I went through a difficult period with a woman who was physically and psychologically violent and abusive. After a protracted and destructive separation, this woman ran a two-year campaign of social-psychological harassment. Her targets were me; my work and projects; my friends; my sister and her lover, Jane; and Jane's work. I think one of the reasons that I was able to leave the relationship when I did, and survive as well as I did, was because my sister and friends and I had a culture of sisterliness. It allowed us, belatedly but eventually, to be forthright with one another and to comment on things that other lesbians may regard, for ideological reasons, as private. Abusers rely on separating the victim from others and they depend on the laziness or reticence of onlookers, who make no comment or avert their eyes or mumble about the two sides to every story. When you're dealing with a liar and a bully, there aren't two sides. I believe that being part of a "sister-thing" made it hard for the bully to separate me from others who cared about me. I survived thanks to women who insisted on maintaining blunt and unsophisticated sisterly relationships. I was really grateful, too, that there was a trained nurse in the family during this time; Robyn is the main reason why my scarring from trauma is minimal. Her matter-of-fact approach to my physical symptoms helped reduce secondary symptoms, and it was incredibly empowering to have that kind of support. It was okay for me to trust her and be "looked after" by her, at a time when my usual clues about whom to trust had been invalidated. The other thing about an abusive experience with a liar is that you're not sure what's true any more and you feel that you have to come up with proof of the abuse. With my sister and sister-friends, I didn't need to prove anything. What happened to me was real to them, too, and they kept me from disappearing.

Robyn's partner, Jane, and I have our own friendship and connection, in addition to the connection I have with them as partners. That's a first for me, and it's wonderful. I know I'd be friends with Jane anyway, regardless of her connection to Robyn, because I like her.

In 1992, Robyn and I went into business together and formed a registered company to run a feminist bookshop called "The Murphy Sisters." In 1993, we opened a second shop called "Sisters by the Sea." Robyn works at Murphy Sisters' and I work at Sisters by the Sea. I have found it to be both a good thing and a hard thing to work in a team with my sister. I entertain the notion that, unlike our straight sisters who reproduce, we lesbians re-create a culture of sisterhood among women. I like the idea of developing a women's economy. Putting these ideas into practice has been difficult, though, in the absence of authentic feminist or lesbian theory and in the absence of practical models. On the other hand, it's been difficult to avoid the confusion (and, at times, sabotage) created by promulgators of ideas from redundant ideologies, imported from the British or American models, about work and business and feminism. They don't reflect Australian realities about income and class and power and women's work — including, realities about women who work for themselves and for other women in an economically sustainable way. Robyn and I are lucky; in our partnership, we can trust each other one-hundred percent, and we have great friends who are good thinkers and who have practical resources. Together, we've developed ways of talking about being in business, about women's work and worth, about mutual respect, about ethics and violence, about rights to property or prosperity, about roles and boundaries in the community and about creating a woman-primary place.

My brief experience in small business has already shown that these ideas are not particularly attractive to coalitionists or the chic (who seem to require boyfriends or brothers in order to go anywhere with their ideas) or with the UK-imported socialists or the big-business high-fliers. But having a woman and sisterly focus at Sisters Bookshops still appeals to a lot of lesbians, despite the current push for diversity in, and tolerance of, anti-lesbianisms.

I know that my relationship with my lesbian sister sets a standard for my expectations of relationships with other lesbians: I believe that I was born into my lesbian relationship; that I have a right to it; and that, at some level, I don't have to earn it — it's part of my birthright and my life story. I do have to nurture it, but I don't have to be precious about it. That would be a good thing to spread around to all the sisters: If you weren't born with a sister-lesbian, you can always adopt one.

Robyn

Being frightened, being hit by nuns, crying, wetting my bed, wanting my mother, being small: these are my earliest recollections of childhood and of the religion that entered my life at the age of six. It was then that Anne-Marie, my older (by two years) lesbian sister, and I were sent to a Catholic boarding school in Port Lincoln, South Australia.

My mother died in November 1962, at the age of thirty-seven, while giving birth to her fifth child — my youngest sister, Therese. Three months later, in February 1963, Anne-Marie and I were "sent off" to boarding school. It was here I spent the next ten years of my life. We were the only girls of primary-school age among all the other boarders, so we grew up with older girls and women around us. My newborn sister, Therese, was adopted by my mother's oldest sister, Madge, who had not had any children of her own. Madge lived in Port Lincoln, too, so from a very early age I was aware I had another sister (who turned out to be heterosexual), but I did not have access to her in the usual sense. It was not until we were both in our twenties that we developed any relationship at all.

Our teachers and "protectors" were nuns — women in big brown habits. I remember washing my wet bedsheets with my sister, and I would have seen Anne-Marie every day but I can't remember be-friending her. In fact, holidays were spent screeching and scratching at each other — we fought more often than we were friends. We didn't compete for friends or affection within the family because there was none to get — our father was a non-parent. My older sister, Veronica, was fourteen when our mother died, and she took on the role of parent to some degree, but she lived back on the farm, and most of our lives was spent at the boarding school. I did not develop any significant-other relationships until adolescence, and that was with a school friend of my own age.

From the moment I entered the grounds of the school it was Latin Mass, with gloves and hats, every day at 7:00 a.m. — and twice on Sundays — plus, of course, benediction, novena, and many other cere-monies thrown in every week. I was beaten at least twice a week for such crimes as turning around in church, improperly cleaned shoes, spelling errors, and talking during study time. Even though we were saturated with religion, I did not have a deep faith and had no sense of my mother being present in spirit; rather, I had a sense of her being talked about and her death being a tragedy within our small community.

Treats were rare. My sister and I celebrated our birthdays in the same week and were each given a baby cupcake to mark the occasion. I remember that Therese was brought to the convent on such occasions and sat in the highchair — her birthday was also in the same week — but it was as if she was unreachable. You could look, but not touch. Madge was extremely protective of her and I always felt very lucky to see her.

In general, Anne-Marie and I were not encouraged to have any personality or individuality during our school life. At times, we were seen by the nuns as crossing the boundaries of acceptable behaviour for girls: playing marbles was not a part of that behaviour and beating the boys — which Anne-Marie was capable of doing — definitely wasn't acceptable. We were both good at sport and, as we grew into our teens, we often competed against each other in hot-tempered matches. This was the extent of our similarities during our school days. Even our appearance was different: Anne-Marie was dark, I was fair. Anne-Marie read a lot more than me and was extremely smart.

By the end of my school days, I had a sense of being "girl-cen-tred." Males were absent from my everyday experience, except for the all-powerful priest or bishop. I remember being infatuated with a nun while still at school — I used to talk to her about lots of things. I regarded her as a mentor and a stabilizing adult influence. I even kept in touch with her after she left the convent and got married. I didn't identify my attraction to her as anything sexual at the time, but I'm sure that's what it was. She wasn't a gym teacher, but the ingredients were definitely part of the same lesbian-identifying recipe.

In 1972, when I was still at school in Port Lincoln and Anne-Marie was doing her first year of teacher's training in Adelaide (the capital of South Australia), Anne-Marie had a very close friendship with a nun named Sister Mary, who died tragically. I remember being woken up in the middle of the night by the police, who wanted me to get hold of Dad. I listened in the kitchen and heard that Anne-Marie had been in a car accident with this nun and that the nun had been killed.

The next morning I made arrangements to fly to Adelaide and visit Anne-Marie in the hospital. I didn't recognize her: she was black and blue, her face was smashed up, she had wires coming out of her mouth and her jaw was wired. Anne-Marie had received permission from the hospital to go to the funeral, with medical supervision. Our sister Veronica, who was a registered nurse, and I accompanied her. The funeral was at a huge city church, and hundreds of nuns attended it. Anne-Marie asked me to take her up in the wheelchair to the open coffin to talk to the body of Sister Mary and to give her a flower. I remember that Sister Mary didn't have any marks on her. Anne-Marie was calm as she talked to her, but she had tears splashing down her face. The whole congregation was quiet and waited for Anne-Marie to say her good-bye. It was then that I really detected the deep intimacy of Anne-Marie's friendship with Sister Mary.

As soon as I left school in 1974, Anne-Marie and I started to socialize together and began to know each other as adults. We had stopped fighting, and even shared a house with two other women in 1974-75. I was doing my nursing training, and Anne-Marie was completing her teacher's training. "Robyn is the nurse and Anne-Marie is the teacher" — that was how we were identified and described.

We were both becoming feminists and quite politically aware — both in our lifestyle and through our reading. Lesbianism didn't feature in the discussions, but I was certainly aware that I was not heterosexual; I couldn't see a future in it, really. I got my first motorbike during that time — I remember that clearly!

For the first time, Anne-Marie and I were forming our own social groups and forging our own personalities — we were becoming true individuals. Anne-Marie was developing into a thinker and academic, whereas I was more interested in sports and was developing my own political awareness.

I spent three years in Adelaide, then went back to Port Lincoln to be the adult caretaker of our sister Therese, who was still in school. The previous year, Anne-Marie had returned to Port Lincoln to do the same thing. Madge had died two years before, so Therese had gone from a secure loving home to quite a dysfunctional one. She was abused by our father very soon after Madge's death, and this went on for five years before she nearly killed him with a knife one night as she tried to defend herself. Although she had called out for help from other adults as soon as the abuse had started happening, nothing was done until she did it herself.

It was while I was in Port Lincoln in 1978, working as a nursing sister, that I had my first lesbian relationship. My first casualty was a nurse! When I realized I was a lesbian, I thought, "This is fantastic. Anne-Marie should know about this — if anyone should be lesbian, it's Anne-Marie!" I was twenty-two by that time and had already identified as a feminist for a number of years.

My relationship was a broom-closeted one. My girlfriend was one of triplet girls, so imagine the dynamics in that sibling relationship! She was also an identical twin within the triplet union. I didn't see much of Anne-Marie at that time, since she was still in Adelaide, but I was busting to tell her of my adventures as a new member of the glorious species of lesbiana magnificata. In the end, though, I decided that the closet was safer.

In 1979, I travelled overseas to England, on a trip that would last for two years. My closeted girlfriend and I spent the first year in a two-bedroom flat with eight other women, including two of my lover's sisters. A year and a half later, Anne-Marie came to London. Within fifteen minutes of her arrival, I guessed that she was in a lesbian relationship, too; it was the way she spoke about her "friend" (whom I also knew). I was very excited, but nothing was said until six months later, at Heathrow Airport, just before Anne-Marie departed for Australia. We came out to each other just before the final boarding call — lousy timing! There we were in Heathrow Airport, yelling and whooping with delight, and five minutes later she flew back to Australia. We didn't see each other for another six months, when I, too, returned home at last. That was fifteen years ago.

Today, we are both lesbian feminists and have both contributed to our community through such ventures as lesbian publications, lesbian studies, lesbian conferences, International Women's Day activities and, of course, our two feminist bookshops — Murphy Sisters Bookshop and Sisters By the Sea — which we bought and set up in 1992 and 1993, respectively. Everyone — except our lovers — confuses each of us with the other. We share a business, so we're seen together a lot, we sound alike on the phone and, of course, we both love women. We both hate mornings and love late nights. We have both had relationships with identical twins, married women coming out, and lipstick lesbians! But we are still different in a lot of ways, too. I like playing sports, Anne-Marie likes watching them. I like cats, she likes dogs. Anne-Marie is an informed, talented and extremely witty speaker and is frequently invited to give lectures; I go along and take the photos, having worked for some time as a professional photographer. Furthermore, I'm taller, I'm a bit younger and I *came out first!*

Our relationship today is very business-oriented, except when we get to take a holiday. Our talents lie in different areas, which often leads to lively discussions. Anne-Marie has the ability to soothe and calm me down when I am at the end of my tether and ready to scream because of "a hard day at the office." She has the ability to analyze situations and can guide and assist me in dealing with problems, issues or difficulties. We both aspire to provide our lesbian and feminist community with bookshops that are reflections of lesbian energy, talent and skill. Between us, we have a vast knowledge of the literature, resources and networks that exist for the benefit of lesbians and women. Through our work, we are able to offer and promote books about women's history, spirituality, theory, theology and lives in other countries. We can provide non-sexist and culturally inclusive books for children of all ages and seek to expose children and adults alike to books about Australian Aboriginal culture.

We do share friends, but definitely not lovers. We attract, and are attracted to, different types of women. I would dread to think of the consequences of being attracted to the same women — those sort of sparks flying about in our lives would definitely lead to spontaneous combustion.

Our relationship has evolved from our childhood vision of each other as strangers, to our adolescence as girlfriends, to our adult partnership, where I think: "Yikes, what would it be like *not to have* a lesbian sister." I think it would feel very strange to be without my lesbian sister. I also know how envious other dykes are when they discover I have a lesbian sister. This year, Anne-Marie and I celebrated the beginning of our fourth year in feminist bookselling. And now, at age thirty-eight, I am a few months older than my mother was when she died giving birth. I am convinced, from what I remember of her and from what I have been told by many of her peers over the years, that she was a proud woman — just like her two lesbian daughters.

Sharon Washington
and Sändra Washington

IRENE YOUNG

Left: Sharon   Right: Sändra

A Song in
Two Keys

Sharon

I am often asked about what it is like to be a twin. Well, being a twin is truly all that I/we know. Why is the question never turned around and framed as: What's it like to be a singlet? On the simplest level, I can answer that I always had a playmate growing up. As I reflect on my life experience, I'm not sure if it is something I share with all or most twins — or even with Sändra … It's just mine.

Throughout my high-school and college-undergraduate years, any time I was asked to write my biography I found it difficult to speak in the singular first person until I was reflecting on my experiences from sixteen years of age onwards. When I think of my relationship to my twin over time, there are particular memories that illustrate our shared experiences and feelings and the character of our relationship. The following vignettes capture the character of our relationship with each other across our lifespan, and our relationship with families, friends and lovers over time.

When we were brought home from the hospital, Sändra and I were placed in two separate cribs. Our mom tells stories of hearing a thump, thump, thump from upstairs, seemingly from our room. When she would walk into the bedroom to investigate, she would find Sändra and me rocking our respective cribs to get closer to each other and trying to pull ourselves up and over the crib bars. Seeing this behaviour, she worried that one or both of us would eventually hurt ourselves by successfully scaling the crib rails and plunging to the floor. Her response was to put us both in the same crib, head to toe, where, she said, we immediately started sucking on each other's toes and fell fast asleep.

By the time we were three or four years of age, our personalities were set. We were intent on breaking new territory and going where no one had gone before — a trait characterized well by the "trash can on the hill" episode. Sändra and I were fascinated by anything that was the right size for crawling into — especially small things. So it was hardly surprising that the tall, cylinder trash can became a source of wonder for us. Through scientific inquiry, we discovered its rolling properties and deduced that a fun ride could be had if one of us crawled inside and her co-experimenter gave the contraption a little push. Well, from there it was but a small leap to the front hill for a much bigger ride. I, of course, went first (a decision that combined my impetuousness and Sändra's suggestion) and, with total trust in the outcome, I crawled in, got the initial push from Sändra and rolled down a steep and bumpy hill into the ditch and up the other side right across the road — all within sight of our father, who was driving home from work and wondering what his trash can was doing out in the road, and why one of his children was inside!

Growing up, Sändra and I were teased by our cousins and some of our friends for not fighting with each other. They said it was unnatural and that all siblings did it. They would try to get us to fight with or yell at each other, but we never did until we were in our late teens. When it happened, I remember being surprised, hurt, angry and scared. Over time I/we have become more comfortable fighting and have learned to do so without all the drama of adolescent and young-adult angst.

I remember that, in seventh grade, I felt betrayed by my friends — and especially Sändra — when they began to act "boy crazy." I felt as though they were changing and who they were was disappearing. I didn't understand the purpose of acting stupid so boys would like them. In the fall of tenth grade, I again felt betrayal, disgust and hurt — this time over Sändra's seeming "spinelessness" in her interactions with a senior girl, B. I remember calling Sändra out of some after-school club meeting and yelling at her and B. I was angry because I felt that Sändra was acting like a puppet, and I told B. that she was the puppeteer and that every time she pulled a string Sändra did whatever she wanted. I remember feeling angry and sad … I now see that they were a couple, but back then I didn't even have words to describe their relationship. I just knew I didn't like the loss of Sändra.

Looking back on my earlier years, I also remember at least one experience which was clearly about me consciously looking at my life and my social identities in terms of race and class. I was in graduate school in Ohio and I remember writing a poem to my parents, talking about incidents that occurred when I was young, and that illustrated a desire to be white: me wanting to visit Switzerland and attend a boarding school; Sändra and I, in the second grade, tying yellow and orange towels to our heads and pretending we had "white people's hair"; et cetera. I acknowledged the hurt this rejection of my blackness must have caused them. It was at this time that I was beginning to name the internalized racism I had learned in a society which nurtures the self-hatred of blackness.

In junior high and high school, I remember thinking that having my white friends say "I don't see you as black but white" was a compliment. In college, I remembered those comments and was angry — angry at them, and angry at myself for thinking that it was better to be thought of as white than as black. I knew that they/I weren't/wasn't seeing all of me. At the same time, I felt hurt when other black youths would call me "Oreo" and wouldn't want to play with me. The combination of the two messages said this: "Even though my white friends don't really see me, they like me, while black kids don't see me and don't like me." So I was afraid to interact with other black people for fear of them finding out how "white" I was and rejecting me. I now have a better sense of this process. Reading Beverly Daniel Tatum's book *Assimilation Blues: Black Families in a White Community* clearly illustrated and reflected experiences similar to my own and lessened my feelings of isolation and belief that there were only two of us who had this experience.

In high school, the guidance counsellor tried to urge me to go to vocational school instead of college. In fact, all through elementary school, teachers would tell my mother that one of us couldn't read, couldn't do math, couldn't do … Our parents' response was that we shouldn't believe white people's opinions about us, especially when they contradicted what we thought, felt or wanted to do with our lives. I have harboured the idea of wanting to go back to every teacher in school who said we "couldn't do" and shove my accomplishments in their face.

Positive messages of black pride and history came to us from a series of black-heritage comic books; a black-history board game; having an older brother who made us repeat after him "I'm black and beautiful" and who taught us the song "To Be Young, Gifted and Black"; having week-long summer visits to other relatives' houses, where we would play with more black kids; and going to summer day camp with older cousins.

Sändra and I shared an upbringing that was filled with active pursuits and the message — and practice — of giving things back to the community. This message initially came from our family and was reinforced by the Girl Scouts. Our first home was in a rural area on a very small, post-commercial apple orchard. We spent time in the woods camping, hiking and canoeing with Dad and the family; by the time we joined Girl Scouts in the second grade, we were well on our way to defining our future professional interests in the related fields of recreation and leisure, and the National Park Service (Sharon and Sändra, respectively).

We have both incorporated the practice of giving back to the community in our work within our professions. I am currently teaching in the social-service field of recreation and leisure studies. I help students question the ways in which forms of social oppression impact the delivery of leisure services in the field, and the ways in which they personally perpetuate different forms of oppression. Sändra is helping communities interested in building new trails and green spaces to create committees that are inclusive. Together, we share a career in music and contribute to social and political change in an artistic manner.

I know that my life is a testament to the combined influence of my parents. My mother was a music teacher/guidance counsellor/musician who liked to travel and go on adventures, and my father was a community recreation volunteer/outdoor enthusiast/procurement analyst/athlete who always made time to help others. The fact that I am a teacher/musician/outdoor enthusiast/traveller, and am committed to social justice, is clearly the result of balancing my parental influences. Sändra's choices to become an outdoor planner/musician/Girl Scout volunteer/traveller illustrate a similar blending. I feel as though both of us are standing on the shoulders of those who have gone before us in our struggle to continue creating environments that are more inclusive than the ones in which we grew up.

My relationships with the other members of my family have been good. Our brother, Luzern, was twelve and a half years older than us and so he was often one of my and Sändra's caretakers when we were very young. As I grew into my twenties, he was a distant, adored adult. What sticks out in my mind when I recall Luzern is his playfulness with us, the great story adventures he would take us on at bedtime, his activism and involvement with the Black Power Movement, and the fact that he pursued the profession of his choice — acting. Because he died at such a young age (thirty-five), I can only speculate what our relationship would be like today. I know I would be out to him, and I believe he would have been accepting of me. I would probably have begun to spend more time with him as I became increasingly independent.

I know I was Daddy's girl growing up and throughout my twenties. It was very hard on Dad when I told him I was a lesbian, but over the years he certainly came around and was accepting of us in his own way. He was very proud of our music and our educational pursuits. I know that it gave him great pleasure that I was gainfully employed in a secure career, and still doing music, before he died. I will always treasure the memories of Dad taking us canoeing for the first time, letting Sändra and me go camping on our own when we were thirteen, letting me take him horseback riding when I gave riding lessons, coming to our concerts whenever he could, and generally just being there throughout the final part of his life.

In the last several years, my relationship with my mother has blossomed. We chat-it-up on the phone several times a week and take little trips to see each other. I am certain that some of this came about as a result of the death of our dad and Sändra's move to Nebraska to form a life partnership with her lover, D. I truly am enjoying the new sense of closeness to Mom and feel comfortable talking to her about both my professional and my personal life. When I was living temporarily in Northampton, Massachussetts, and told her I was dating, she even suggested I play the field since I wasn't going to be there long!

I have a sense that my relationships with lovers and partners have been affected by my relationship with Sändra. At times, some of my lovers were jealous of the closeness Sändra and I shared and the time we spent together working and as family. I am conscious of the fact that, quite often throughout the years, I would tell Sändra things about my girlfriend that clearly crossed a boundary in the lover relationship; but, in my mind, I could tell Sändra anything and it did not count as betraying a "secret" because it was like telling an extension of myself.

In the last two or three years, we have moved into another stage in the evolution of our relationship. I have been focusing a lot on acknowledging Sändra's feelings as separate from mine, and trying to really believe that, when I feel as though I've let her down, the voice inside of me that says that I am unlovable is not correct. Here's one example of how I was not able to see us as separate: I clearly wanted the two of us to be seen as good; so, if Sändra was angry, I became overly pleasant and congenial. What this behaviour pattern really did was set up a pattern of good one/bad one in others' eyes, which did not serve either one of us well. The clearer I become about myself as an autonomous being, the more I realize that Sändra's opinion is not critical to my acceptance in the world, by others or myself. This, in turn, has allowed me to view Sändra's behaviour and decisions — especially when they do not reflect my own — as perfectly fine and different.

I no longer experience Sändra's relationships with others as a loss to me. I won't say that I don't miss the closeness we used to share as young girls, but I do have an understanding of those relationships as not taking away from me, but as an addition to Sändra — the theory of abundance, in practice!

Sändra

"Hey, twin. Sharon? Or Sändra? I never could tell the two of you apart. I bet sometimes even your parents can't tell the difference. Does your mother or father ever mistake the two of you?"

Sometimes they did. Teachers and acquaintances, and even family members, had difficulty distinguishing Sharon and me from each other, and, although it was just another part of growing up, it got old after a while. So much so, that people who are unable to tell me from my sister never become close friends. The irony is that Sharon and I are never one hundred percent certain who's who in our baby pictures! The most unsettling thing I ever heard about the two of us being twins came out of my mother's mouth: a teasing comment about not being sure, when we were babies, which of us was Sharon and which of us was Sändra. Mom claims that she and Dad just called both of us both names and eventually we each responded to a particular one. I remember feeling discombobulated for a while after she told me this, as if parts of me did not quite fit together.

In some of my memories and dreams from child-hood, I've misplaced who things happened to. This doesn't occur with every event, but it has happens often enough to make me understand how intertwined my existence is with Sharon's. It is almost as if we were more than telepathic — we not only seemed to know what the other was thinking, we seemed to live what was happening to the other. Many of the stories I have from early childhood are really our parents' remembrances. Only Mom and Dad know for certain which of us fell off the sled into the drift. I swear it was me, and Sharon swears it was her. I do remember falling head-first off the back of the sled into a deep pile of snow; I recall the surprise and cold of the snow around my face, and feeling my legs over my head. And, just as well, I remember feeling an emptiness behind me after Sharon fell and I recall turning around to look. It was like having hundreds of out-of-body experiences. These combined memories fill the years until we were ten or eleven, and occur sporadically whenever the two of us spend a lot of intense time together.

So much of my perception of myself is grounded in the idea of counterbalance. Adults outside the family, and our peers, tended to think Sharon and I were completely the same. On the other hand, our parents worked very hard to instill strong individual personalities in us, and they and the extended family tended to polarize our attributes. I remember being given assignments in English class where I was asked to analyze the antagonist and protagonist and explain how they were similar to and different from each other. Well, I feel like everyone outside of Sharon and I used a similar "compare and contrast" model to make a clearer distinction between us for themselves. If Sharon liked blue, then Sändra liked pink; because one likes sports, they must both like sports. I've heard that most people raised with siblings also go through the dividing of traits and attributes among siblings, as if, no matter how many children exist in the family, there can only be no more than one complete person among them. That constant analysis of who I was in relation to Sharon profoundly affects my self-perception and the relationship I have with my sister. I also feel set up to expect dichotomy in the world: right or left, athletic or bookish, and so on. I struggle to remind myself that there is no dichotomy; that it is possible to be both athletic and bookish and butch and femme, and that there are no opposites and no identical beings.

Moving away from home was the best thing that ever happened to me. If I was going to be labelled the independent one, the loner, then off I would go. Okay, so I moved only eight miles away from home —

what wings! But the important thing was that people didn't have to know I was a twin or that, throughout my childhood, I had been only half of a complete person. We can never delete our past, though: people who do not know that I have a sister call me "Sharon." This is very eerie, as if I carry my sister's name on my forehead, or as if my mother's story was true — I may in fact be "Sharon."

While growing up, Sharon and I often shared friends and we always brought a friend along on outings. We loved to go to amusement parks, but sharing a friend was such a bother on those outings because rides were designed for couples. One of us — never the friend — was always the odd one out. On rare occasions, we had a fourth along. After we began to drive, we usually each had a friend who did things with us, but still three was the most common number for social gatherings. Mom and Dad always wanted the two of us to play together and it was easier to arrange things with one friend than with two.

I began writing in middle school as a way to have a piece of myself that was separate from my sister. At the time, I was having difficulty understanding many of my thoughts and feelings. I would cry every day in the girls' bathroom (last stall, beige doors, small green tile squares, individual little sheets of toilet paper in chrome containers) over friends, puberty, my ugliness, the torment of being among unfamiliar students who didn't know that my struggle for acceptance in grade school was supposed to mean that I didn't have to take mean, racist torture all over again. (Sharon and I were two of five black children in elementary school. By middle school, there were six or eight black kids out of two or three hundred students.) In addition, most of my friends had gone stupid over boys, and, thinking I should be doing the same, I embarrassed myself over a shy, skinny kid with dark brown eyes and white skin. Then, in eighth grade, I snuck a look at my school file and read that my favourite teacher, Mrs. Razor from third grade, had labelled me slow, unable to read or spell properly and unsociable. That hurt so badly. I stood there reading, trying not to cry. I was devastated and pissed and humiliated that someone I trusted did not believe I was valuable. I started to keep myself apart, and writing gave me an outlet all the way through high school. I truly believe it kept me sane and alive.

I began to have powerful feelings for my girlfriends from around the time I was in fifth grade. When I was fourteen, I fell madly (quite literally) in love with B., an upperclasswoman in high school. We met on a science trip during the summer of 1975. After thirty-one days of togetherness, we were inseparable. I was passionate about this girl. I had sexual dreams about her, my body ached, my sleep was tortured, and all day, every day, I stared at her. I stared at her in front of friends, the other students on the trip, the teachers. I don't remember Sharon's reaction at the time, but as the term progressed and B. and I went through a soap-opera romance in full view of the entire high school and our parents, I knew Sharon pretty much thought B. was a very bad influence on me. No matter how much my sister questioned me, I didn't tell her the truth of my feelings for B. until much later; and, for whatever reason, Sharon appeared to have forgotten all about it by the time I came out to her at nineteen.

There were several reasons I withheld from Sharon the fact that I was a lesbian. First, she did not especially like my first girlfriend. Second, later in that year or the next, Sharon clearly stated her feelings about lesbians. We were hanging out with friends, talking about cool girls we knew from different high schools. Someone mentioned that so-and-so was gay, and Sharon piped up, "How disgusting!" I had very nearly outed my first girlfriend (to scout the territory for myself), but immediately shut my mouth. The final incident that strengthened my resolve to keep my lesbianism from Sharon occurred on a Girl Scout trip to the Ozarks. My first girlfriend, B. (in part two of the soap opera), had agreed to come along. We had not spoken to each other in the months since our dramatic break-up. We spent hours sitting next to each other in the van, silently working up the nerve to discuss what was happening between us. Finally, we began to talk. As B. was relaying her feelings about my "goddamn" naïvete during our romance, Sharon over-heard her. She ran over, picked up B. by the collar and slugged her in the face — a not-so-subtle clue for me to keep my closet door closed in front of my sister.

Even Sharon's coming out during our senior year did not change my resolve to keep my privacy. At that point, I was dating a boy (I wanted to go to the school dances in my senior year), so I figured she wouldn't believe me, and I didn't want her thinking I was trying to hone in on her lesbian territory. It was not until I was nineteen that I told Sharon I had been a lesbian since I was fourteen. Her initial response was to suggest to me that I was just following her lead — that I was a copycat lesbian. So I finally proved the fact by kissing a woman full on the mouth, in full view of Sharon, at the drag show we attended for our birthday. (I know there is another story in that line, but I'm not explaining.)

Discussing the relationship and private side of "The Washington Sisters" is an act of monumental proportions for us. Our parents, especially Dad, always stressed the importance of family camaraderie. "Always stand up for your sister. Do not argue or disagree with your sister in front of anyone outside of the family. Family are the only people you can trust." Dad repeated these statements many, many times while we were growing up.

Since my early teens, I have tried to have a sense of "otherness" and a separation from the twin identity. The years of telepathic closeness have filled up any need that I might have to know everything about another human being and I envy siblings who seem to have easy-going, intimate relationships.

I still don't feel as though I've been able to reconcile my desire for a close relationship with my sister with my need for independence. I fear I will not measure up to my sister's expectations of what an adult twin relationship should be. Sharon and my relationship continues to evolve, from an all-encompassing togetherness to an emotional struggle for independence and respect.

Left: Sharon   Right: Sandra

Sharon

Sändra

TO SAPPHO, MY SISTER

Theresa Corrigan
and Anne Corrigan

Theresa

Anne

Harmonic
Convergence

Theresa and Anne

Theresa's story:

On May 2, 1954, I began a journey that now seems like the most significant of my life: the journey into sisterhood. I was an ill-prepared traveller. For five years I had been a solitary child, and I liked it that way. I lived in a child's paradise — a farm in Pennsylvania with thirty acres of everything I could want: thirty-five cats, all named and known; Smokey the bird dog; a barn with a loft so high I could fly off it into soft hay; fields full of rabbit holes that were occupied in spring; the creek that ended in the back forty at a dump — a wonderful place for creative concoctions, blends of half-empty bottles, medicinal magic; and, most important of all, a magnificent house — red brick with towering pillared porch. This is the archetypal house that still inhabits my dreams. It had an attic filled with boxes of memories, musty odours of old photographs and Christmas ornaments; it had a cellar that smelled of sweet rain all year long. Most of all, I remember the kitchen. It was the only room heated in winter, and it was there that I coloured while Mommy cooked the plain and sumptuous meals from her Southern heritage; it was there in the warmth that I read the Dr. Doolittle stories and talked to the animals while she canned. This was my world. Who needed a sister?

Mother tells me they prepared me for Anne's arrival, but I have no recollection of a pregnant mother. I only remember the day she got out of the old black Oldsmobile, carrying her bundle of joy. I reluctantly peered under the blankets, and in my little mind I knew this was a bundle of trouble. I had a feeling there would only be room for one, and Anne seemed to be the one. She was Mommy's baby. Who was I? I was soon to be Daddy's big girl, who didn't make a fuss or cry, who was always strong and smart, who didn't act like a Momma's baby. I was not happy.

I was even less happy when, shortly after Anne's arrival, I was sent to school. Here was my proof that there was only room for one. Well, I had other ideas. I ran mysterious fevers that abruptly lowered when I was released from school; I spent weeks in the hospital with a body weakened by depression. Denied open rebellion by a father who demanded quiet obedience, I chose the only solution I could — to be the sick baby. Unfortunately, every virus or bacteria that I could find hit little Anne even harder. She was always the sicker baby. Studies of sibling rivalry find that sisters will often tacitly choose different arenas in which to excel or compete in order to maintain their self-esteem. I learned this lesson quite young. After three hospital stays, I stopped being sick and began to excel at school.

Despite my complaints, Mother insisted that we keep Anne, and we settled into a typical sister relationship: She adored me and I tolerated her (although I would fight anyone who picked on her). Father was in the army and we travelled together to Ethiopia, then to Germany, on to a little German town in Illinois, then to California (first San Jose, then to Stockton, finally to Sacramento for me and San Diego for Anne).

Although we moved to the same places, Anne and I rarely travelled the same paths. Once in school, Anne became the extrovert, always gathering a band of boys as her cohorts. I found my friends in books and animals. Anne was the athlete, active and usually outside; I was the recluse, spending hours hiding somewhere with Nancy Drew. Although we both did well in school, Anne hated Mondays because they marked an end to freedom; I still cherish the smell of new pencils and books and the memories of school they represent. We shared little in common — or so it seemed during childhood.

As the older sister, I was both bully and rebel. Anne suffered mercilessly from my teasing and taunting. When I kicked the nail-biting habit by growing inordinately long nails, I would sink them into her arm and dare her to tattle, one of her favourite activities. Many of our childhood conversations went like this:

T: You better not tell about (fill in the blank).
A: I'm going to tell Mother.
T: I'll hurt you.
A: *Mother*!!!
T: You're gonna get it now.
A: (Sounds of screaming.)

Sound familiar? We were not unlike many siblings who rivalled for Mother's attention and frequently hid from Father's. That rivalry prevented us from achieving any untainted intimacy until I came out.

I was also the rebel. I became involved in the anti-Vietnam War Movement in high school, began using drugs and alcohol, got involved in a sexual relationship with a man my first year in college and sought revolutionary political thought (in short, I became a hippie). As I did each of these things, I told my mother what I was doing. Fortunately, she was able to keep her dread and fear sufficiently in check in front of me to keep the lines of communication open. Unfortunately, Anne, because she was still living at home, was often witness to Mother's private reactions. Anne learned early to keep her rebellions to herself. So, while I was brazen in my forays into self-discovery, Anne learned secrecy. She did most of what I had done, but no one in the family knew, including me.

I came out at the age of twenty. Like most of us, in hindsight I can see the seeds of my lesbian identity. From my third-grade crush on Mrs. Larson, to my eighth-grade adoration of Mrs. Miller, to my adolescent passion for Elizabeth Taylor, my tapestry was weaving itself, but I hadn't a clue because, in my world, "queer" was a term reserved for people you didn't like. I did not have a language or concept for homosexuality until I went to college and met one of my best friends, a gay male English professor. Through my relationship with Charles, I acquainted myself with a gay reality and began to question my own sexuality. But it was a year into our friendship before I came out.

It happened in 1971. Through Susan, a friend of Charles' who became my lover, I was introduced into a whole new world, a world in which I felt safe and accepted. I loved it. I joined the pool team, spent nearly every night in the bar and slept with lots of women for the sheer joy and excitement of it. Though Susan and I did not remain lovers, we continued to be pals.

It was about six months later that I met the first woman I was to fall in love with and I began to feel the need to tell my family. I began by laying a foundation, talking to Mother about gay friends I had and discussing the general topic of homosexuality. But she didn't appear to be picking up on the signals. After a few months of these generic conversations, I gave up. My fear got the better of me and I decided that this would be one area of my life that my family wouldn't know about.

When I finally came out to Mother, it was unplanned. I was home for a visit when Pop made some disparaging remark at the dinner table about gays. I left the table in tears, and Mother followed me back to the bedroom. She said, "I know what is bothering you; you're afraid you're a homosexual, aren't you?"

"No, I know I am," I said. "That's not the problem. I'm in love and I'm afraid she's not in love with me."

From there, our conversation degenerated into every typical negative parental response. Mother finally said I should leave in the morning. I was devastated and decided to go. But I wanted to talk to Anne before I left town. I knew that if she didn't hear it from me, she couldn't begin to understand what was happening for me, and I wanted her to know my feelings.

Anne's story:

I was sixteen when I found out that my sister was a lesbian. I was sitting in my sophomore biology class. Luckily the room was in the front of the school and I could see Theresa as she crossed the front lawn. I left class to meet her. I had no idea what was going on, but, the night before, she and Mother had been talking for hours in private. I could tell they both had been crying, but neither of them offered an explanation that night or the next morning.

Theresa told me that she was in love with another woman. She explained that she was happy being a lesbian, even though Mother would probably tell me it was a sin. I cried. At the time I had no clue why I was crying, other than that the people I cared most about were upset. (I think now that I was terrified of losing my family. This seemed to be something big enough to break the bond between Theresa and Mother, which I had perceived as indestructible; it seemed like something that wouldn't go away if we just ignored it. I feared that Theresa would leave forever. She had already gone away to college, and each year she came home less often. Now she had even more reason to stay away.)

As much as Theresa wanted me to understand her that day, I did not. Lesbians were the women my mother knew in the army who were good workers but not people you wanted to socialize with. My English teacher was said to be a lesbian because she had never married and had lived with the same woman for years. But she wasn't someone I really knew or cared to know. Now, here was my sister — a lesbian. I knew that I loved her, so whatever she was had to be okay, but it was scary.

That afternoon, I arrived home to find Mother crying. She said she just couldn't believe that Theresa was a lesbian and that she would never be able to accept it in her heart. She would pray for Theresa to change. But, oddly, in the midst of all this, Mother also told me that I should love my sister, that we should be close and be able to rely on each other throughout our lives. I felt she was telling me that, even if she couldn't deal with the situation herself, I should try to deal with it in order to keep my relationship with Theresa and to help maintain Theresa's connection to the family.

It was weeks later before Theresa finally called to talk to Mother. After that conversation, Mother asked me if I wanted to go to visit Theresa in Sacramento; Theresa had requested that I come up to see her. I missed her and definitely wanted to go, so I went the next weekend. After I arrived and met Theresa's lover, I immediately found some private place to cry in my confusion. I was afraid of what her lover would think of me and was sure she thought I was a crazy little kid. I still don't remember much of that weekend, but it was the beginning of many more visits. (I realize now that this really was the beginning of my adult relationship with Theresa.)

From that time on, my high-school days were schizophrenic. I was a homophobic, heterosexual teenager among my friends in Stockton, and an asexual little sister in Sacramento. Still, I went to Sacramento as often as I could because I loved my time with Theresa and her friends. These women were funny, strong, outspoken, and certainly knew how to have a good time. I felt special hanging out with older women. They would take me to dances and sneak me into the bar. We shot pool, drank beer, and soon I felt that I belonged. (I never knew until later that Theresa had warned her friends to keep their hands off her little sister. I think she felt the need to "protect" me for Mother's sake.)

In spite of my comfort in Sacramento, I never shared any of my Sacramento experiences with my friends at home or told any of them that my sister was a lesbian. I was afraid of their responses. In Stockton, I drank, did drugs and joined my friends in occasionally cruising by the only gay bar in town, yelling "Queer" at the people standing outside. I assumed that my friends and I were heterosexual. We dated the appropriate sex and acted the part well enough, but obviously some of us were not as sure as we had thought. By the time we were a year out of high school, all but one of us had come out.

In 1972, I left home, kicking and screaming, to go to college in San Diego. The dorm to which I was assigned housed most of the sorority overflow and I couldn't relate to these women. Two other women with whom I shared a suite were my saving grace. My roommate and I hit it off from the start — we were two would-be hippies. We actually had matching Indian-print bedspreads. The other woman, Sara, was a hippie who shared her room with her boyfriend (on the sly). I thought she was beautiful and very cool.

That first semester I was ready to go home and finish my education at the local junior college. I missed my parents, my sister and the dogs, but I had promised to tough it out for a year. Mom said that if I didn't like it I could come home. But, by the end of the first year, I didn't want to. My second semester turned out to be a six-month courtship for Sara and me. While we were getting to know each other, I was also still involved with a high-school boyfriend who now lived in Laguna Beach, and I would occasionally spend the weekend with him. (He announced his bisexuality one night, after telling me that he thought I was in love with Sara. Later I found out that he was gay and had been having affairs with men throughout our high-school years.)

Sara and I actually spent a lot of time with her boyfriend, but the time we had alone became more and more valuable. She was the first friend to whom I talked about my sister being a lesbian. I told her about my trips to Sacramento and she understood. Late one night she knocked on my door and proceeded to tell me about a sexual dream she had had about me. I was terrified and finally asked her to leave. I had been spending plenty of time among lesbians and I had already had crushes on some of my girlfriends, but this was new and scary. It involved acknowledging my feelings. Sara and I had often found excuses to touch each other, but we had never talked about our feelings.

Shortly after that night, we became lovers. Her boyfriend knew what was happening and assumed that we would all be lovers. He certainly was surprised when she told him to leave. I was involved with Sara for nearly a year before I told Theresa about my relationship. I told her then only because Sara and I were breaking up. I was heartbroken and phoned Theresa for comfort. I said I was in trouble. (She told me later that she had thought that I was either pregnant or busted; it had not occurred to her that I might be a lesbian.) When she questioned me, I told her I was breaking up with my lover. Something in my tone alerted her that my lover might not be a man. She said, "Who is your lover?"

"Sara," I replied.

She told me to get a flight to Sacramento the next day and she would take care of me. That was the start of many trips like that. Every failed relationship has ended with me calling Theresa. Her response has always been the same: "Get on a plane as soon as you can. I'll be waiting for you."

I waited to tell Theresa that I was a lesbian because I wanted to know that it was my decision and that I wasn't just following in her footsteps. I grew up hearing my parents say "You just want to do everything your sister does." In fact, one of my childhood nicknames was "MeToo." I had never felt such intense emotions and I knew they were real, but I needed time to reassure myself. I didn't want anyone else taking away my coming out. When I finally was comfortable with myself as a lesbian, the question of Theresa's involvement in my process didn't matter. I thank her now for introducing me to the life. I never told Mother because I didn't want her to die — she had made this threat several times. I was afraid that, if she knew she had a track record of two for two, her guilt as a "failed parent" would overwhelm her.

Theresa's story:

My immediate reaction to Anne's revelation was dread. All I could think of was Mother's hysteria; I had turned my sister into "one of those." By this time, Mother and I had reached a truce. She said she would never accept my "lifestyle" but she loved me and didn't want to lose our connection. I said I would never live a lie for her or anyone else, but that I loved her, too. I promised not to put myself in a situation that would "out" her. Now I was faced with being responsible for taking my sister down the path of sin with me. Anne had never been as open as I was with Mother, and she had painfully watched Mother's reaction to my sexuality, so she didn't feel the same compulsion to share her new life with the folks. We mutually decided that I would be the only open lesbian in the family. (Pop died eight years ago and Ma has mellowed over time, so the issue of secrecy seems less compelling, but Anne has still chosen not to openly discuss her relationships. We are both convinced that Ma knows, but she makes it clear that she would like to keep the knowing unconscious. Anne does not lie, she merely omits.)

But even as I felt the dread, I also knew that our paths were converging. The understanding that I had hoped would occur a few years earlier was now imminent — not just because Anne loved me and wanted to understand, but because lesbianism was part of her being as well. But Anne was still my baby sister and it would take several more years for me to rid myself of protectiveness toward her and power over her.

Anne always allowed me to care for her when she was upset. I was the one she turned to when her life was falling apart, who never feared her anger, who could see into her moods and force her to open up. I was learning to see her as a person, but I was still locked into my big-sister role. I didn't allow her the same access to me. I frequently went to San Diego to rest and recuperate from life's kicks in the teeth, but I rarely shared my deepest feelings. I also still exercised the power I knew I had from childhood to get Anne to do what I wanted. I would whine or cajole whenever she asserted her will, and I usually won. I began to realize, however, that winning in the short run was losing me what I needed most from her — a closeness that required her assertion of will, her independence from me, her establishment of a self that could defy my power. But these developments required many more years of pushing each other and ourselves to change.

Anne's story:

I recovered from my first major heartbreak with the help of Theresa and her friends. Theresa's enforcement of a "hands off" policy ended with my coming out, and Sacramento became my playground — a wonderful place to have affairs. I had not been out during my relationship with Sara and now felt the need to establish my lesbian identity in both Sacramento and San Diego. In school, I began taking Women's Studies courses. I joined the Women's Bookstore Collective and started volunteering. Through the store, I met and became friends with many lesbians, some of whom are still a part of my extended family. It was a time of protest marches, rallies, concerts, hanging out at the women's coffee house and playing basketball and softball with my new dyke friends. I met Paula, my next lover, in a Women's Literature class. This time, I shared my feelings with Theresa.

Paula and I were lovers for eight years. During that time, Theresa and Paula became good friends, something I now know to be unique in my life. Of all the women that I've been involved with, she was the only one who didn't feel threatened by my relationship with my sister. She understood the inherent differences between lovers and sisters and was never jealous of the intimacy that I was trying to achieve with Theresa. Paula got to know Theresa not just as my sister but as a person she liked and wanted to spend time with.

In turn, San Diego became a refuge for Theresa when her life seemed too complicated. With us she found a place where she could relax, play and just be silly. We had wonderful times together.

When Paula and I finally broke up, I turned to Theresa for solace. Unfortunately, Theresa was also the person to whom Paula turned, and I had to learn how to share my sister with an ex-lover. It worked because I knew that I could trust Theresa to be honest with me, to be my confidante and to respect boundaries, even though it was the most difficult of my break-ups for Theresa to watch. It meant the loss of a part of her family. I was well into my next relationship before she gave up the hope that Paula and I would get back together again.

Theresa's story:

Paula was my favourite of all Anne's lovers before and since. I was Paula's confidante and she talked more freely with me about her relationship with Anne than Anne did. Their break-up was almost harder on me than on either of them.

With the exception of Paula, our lovers have usually had difficulty with our relationship and have been jealous of the bond between us.

Anne's last serious lover used to complain that I was more important to Anne than she was. I told her that comparisons were useless, at best, and potentially destructive; if she insisted on ranking us, she would lose. My bond with Anne and our lover relationships are like apples and oranges. Even though both of us have had committed relationships that we thought would last forever, we've also known for the past twenty years that our sister allegiance could not be seriously challenged.

It was during Anne's relationship with Paula I began to learn how to rein in my power over Anne — power that I had exercised over little things, like asking her to wait on me, as well as big things, like life decisions. I also stopped taking Anne for granted. I had always known that I could count on Anne's adoration to let me get away with things I wouldn't do to others. Now I cherish her constancy and realize that it doesn't just come with the big-sister territory; it has to be nurtured and grown. I've spent the last ten years valuing that special bond, realizing what a gift it is.

The real turning point in our relationship happened about ten years ago. I had spent five years with my lover at the time, Trina, believing that this was "the one." I was happy and secure like I had never been before with a lover, and commingled my life with Trina's in ways that I had always resisted. It was a glorious time of contentment and trust. But it ended like an explosion in my face. Trina had an affair with a mutual friend and, after months of agony on my part, and confusion and deception on hers, she left. Her departure triggered such old, deep wounds in me that I became suicidal and self-destructive. I had always restrained my pain in front of Anne, thinking that she couldn't handle it. She knew very little of my frightening bouts with depression and agoraphobia. She, like most other people, knew me as strong and capable and always able to handle my own life. But, this time, I had no choice. Reaching out to Anne felt like one of my only chances for survival. I had to risk allowing her to see me out of control.

Anne's story:

My next relationship after Paula was turbulent from the beginning. I met Maggie while she was still married, but we were attracted to each other immediately. Against my better judgment and the advice of my sister and friends, I became involved with her. I was hopelessly in love and passionately in lust, yet neither of us found security in the other. We drank throughout our entire five-year relationship. She was extremely needy of my time and attention, and from the beginning saw Theresa as a threat. The time the three of us spent together was always tense, and usually ended in fights between Maggie and me. Maggie's jealousy over Theresa eventually became one of the deciding factors in the relationship's demise.

Two years into my relationship with Maggie, Theresa called one night in misery. She had discovered that her lover, Trina, was having an affair but still had hope that they would be able to recover their lives if given some time and distance. Theresa had always been available to me when I needed her and I wanted to be able to do the same for her. She came to visit me and I don't think that I have ever seen her so frightened and vulnerable. She was my big sister, the one that I had looked to for strength, the one I knew would always have the answer for everything. Now she appeared to be falling apart and was unsure of anything that she did. Eventually, Theresa left San Diego early on Trina's request — Trina had called to tell her that she missed her and didn't want to lose her. I turned to Maggie for support and found none. For her, Theresa was an intrusion on our relationship and she seemed to have no understanding of my feelings.

For the next few months Theresa and I called each other regularly to check up. She and Trina had started therapy together and Theresa sounded more sure of herself and her relationship. I wanted to believe that she was all right because I was scared of her vulnerability. So scared, in fact, that I didn't take her seriously when she called one night and asked me to come to Sacramento. Trina had lied about stopping her affair and had finally decided to leave Theresa for her new lover. I told Theresa that I would come but I needed a few days to get ready. A few hours later I got another call, this time from Paula. She had just spoken with Theresa and knew that I had better get to Sacramento the next day or I might not have a sister to go to. Theresa had reached out to Paula because they had a history of sharing painful life experiences and they were very similar in their modes of self-destruction. Paula broke through my denial, and I was on a plane to Sacramento the next morning.

I was still not prepared for what happened in the next week. Theresa had never discussed the seriousness of her depressions with me. I'm not sure that she trusted me to understand them and continue to love her. Our roles as big sister and little sister had been set for years and neither one of us knew for certain what would happen to our relationship if they changed. Our roles did change in that week and have continued to change ever since.

During that week, I watched over Theresa, listened to her, held her when she needed to be held and loved her. In the beginning I wasn't sure I could do it. On one particularly hard day, we were sitting in the living room when she suddenly put her fist through a glass-top table and simultaneously tossed a metal cup through one of her fish tanks. Theresa yelled at me to get a bucket for the fish and, as I returned, I noticed that she was holding a piece of glass. I sat down on the couch and told her that I loved her and that if she needed to hurt herself, or even kill herself, I would try to understand but I would not watch. She gave me the piece of glass and we cried for a long time. In that moment not only did I know that my love for Theresa was unshakable; I also found a new respect for myself, an inner strength and depth of understanding that I had never known before. Although I was cognizant of Theresa's needs, I had also asserted my own. For me this was an act of setting boundaries that showed me that I could do so without losing Theresa's love. It's actually taken years for me to fully understand Theresa's depression and just as long to overcome my fear of losing her to it. I still am uncomfortable with her moods and haven't quite learned how to let her be in them and not try to "fix" her. But as we talk more, it frightens me less.

My new insights were lost on Maggie. It hurt that she didn't realize what caring for Theresa had meant to me. All she could talk about was my unwillingness to leave Theresa and come home. It was at this point that I emotionally checked out of that relationship, even though, physically, I stayed for a couple more years. Finally, my father's death and Maggie's departure to another relationship, all in a five-month period, sent me running into therapy.

Theresa's story:

The period after my break-up with Trina was a most remarkable time for me. I had never bottomed out so completely, and though I hope never to do it again, I learned some of the most valuable lessons of my life about myself and my friends. But the most significant lesson was giving up control, and my relationship with Anne was the purest exemplification of it. Anne's words when I smashed that table top will rest in my memory forever. She made the most non-controlling and understanding statement I think I've ever heard. My baby sister had given me the most mature and honest of reactions. From that point on, I knew that the balance of power between us was equal and that I could share my burden of pain with her in the same ways that she had always done with me.

In the years that followed, I've been healing not only from that break-up but from childhood issues that it triggered. Anne, too, has been in counselling, learning to open up. Our parallel therapies have provided us adventures into "family patterns." We discuss our insights into Ma and Pop, lover terrain, our coping mechanisms and, most important, our relationship. We still fight sometimes, but we each know the other's buttons and step lightly around them. We usually fight when we're working on a project together. Anne's too nit-picky for my tastes, and I get too bossy at times, but we've learned how to take time-outs. Anne still worries when I'm depressed and thinks I withhold pertinent information about my emotional life. I assure her that my interior life is sometimes best left there, and I will tell her anything that is relevant to her. She's learning to trust that when I say nothing is wrong, I'm not going to spring something on her later and berate her for not noticing. I still get my feelings hurt when she snaps at me, but she's better at asking what's wrong and I'm better at telling her. Anne's insecurities about being the little sister who was taken for granted sometimes get the better of her and she fears that she's not important enough to me, but I don't get impatient with her any longer.

We are remarkably similar, despite what we heard as youngsters. We share the same values, essentially the same life habits (we even have the same notion about the perfectly folded towel — a source of irritation for others in our lives), the same love of animals, the same eating habits (we're both vegetarian because of our love of animals), the same political views, and the same desire for honesty and intimacy. We have different interests: Anne still prefers to be outdoors, digging and planting, while I would rather be at the computer, writing. But Anne's teaching me about plants, and I've managed to keep nearly all the flowers and bushes we planted at my house alive. I encouraged Anne to work on this piece with me even though she has the worst writing phobia I've ever seen. We have different temperaments. I'm easy-going most of the time and rarely erupt; Anne has a quicksilver temper and will explode when something or someone irritates her. But she's over it as fast as it comes on and she's working on managing her temper. We talk about our differences and know how to negotiate around them. In short, we're developing the healthiest relationship either of us has ever had. It's become my model for every other relationship in my life. Now that we know what is possible, neither of us is willing to settle for less.

Our story:

For several years now, we have been planning to live together in the country. Anne is tired of her job as a research scientist and wants to be a landscape designer. She also makes stained-glass pieces and would like the freedom to do her creative work. Theresa would like more time to focus on her writing. We've also discussed running the bookstore together.

For some years this dream remained at the fantasy level, but two years ago Anne underwent successful surgery for breast cancer and that has added a greater urgency to our plans. We've begun to look at houses. Although we love each other, we both require a great deal of solitude and control over our immediate environments, so we're looking for some land with a house and a cottage. Theresa has offered to inhabit the smaller dwelling because house-cleaning is not her favourite activity. We'd like enough land for Anne to have a small nursery.

We're essentially planning to make a life partnership with each other. We've spent many hours discussing the potential problems we may encounter, everything from combining our nineteen animal households to what will happen when or if either of us has a lover. Both of us have been single for a few years, so we haven't had to deal with the proverbial jealousies. But we are both aware that love can happen when one least expects it. We have made a commitment to each other that anyone entering our lives has to be mature and open enough to value our partnership. Who knows? If either of us gets involved with someone, maybe we'll build another dwelling on the property and begin that old lesbians' home we all dream about.

We've developed the kinds of skills and trust required to build a committed relationship and we want to move into old age together. We both want a quiet and peaceful place in which to raise plants, rescue animals, nurture our creativity and grow into wise women.

The paradise that Theresa had as a child on the farm — the one that Anne's presence threatened so many years ago — is now a shared dream of sisterhood. We are on the same path, travellers who have learned to share the journey and count on each other to be there when we look to the side. We are not so naïve as to think that we will be problem-free. We worry how we will continue if something happens to one of us. Both of us are a little afraid of the interdependence. Neither of us is quite ready to give up the securities of our present lives (jobs, homes, immediacy of friends), but our fantasy is now a plan and some day soon it will be upon us. We have a forty-year relationship that has survived every bump in the road. We have worked hard on ourselves and on us. Each day reaps the harvest of that work even as we commit more time and energy to it. All of it was certainly worth the journey.

Left: Theresa   Right: Anne

Caffyn Kelley

Left: Caffyn   Back: Wendy   Right: Their mother, Cynthia

"Family"

Caffyn

Dear Naomi,

Your mother, Wendy, and I grew up by the Red River in Manitoba. It's a long, deep, wide, muddy river, and in winter the ice covers it, three feet thick. Writing this for you, I feel like I'm chopping through ice, trying to get down to the water. Beneath the ice, the river is careful, unending. The past still happens to us. The water murmurs its secrets until the thaw.

Somewhere inside me, memories are still fluid, visceral. As soon as I reach the water, though, it begins to freeze again. Remembrance is stopped; memories freeze when I write them down. But pictures remind me of something.

This is my mother, with your mother in her arms:

danger

Memory: the prairie grass, bright green and growing, a tangle of brambles, the stink of the swamp. Frog croaks; mosquito hums; ducks bustle in the underbrush. Lady's Slipper rests perfect in the mud, pale orange, beside the startling bright blue of the forget-me-nots.

We scramble across the deadfall, singing alternate lines of the same song:

"The worms crawl in."
"The worms crawl out."
"Through your liver ..."
"And out your snout."
"And then you turn ..."
"All slimy green!"
"The pus comes out ..."
"Like whipping cream ..."
"And me without my spoon!"

Two little girls, five and seven years old, deciphering the wild order of life and death. My sister followed me anywhere, combed my hair, bit me when she had a mind to. I didn't care. I was so much older, stronger — though she could not depend on me.

Our relationship was characterized by petty jealousies, deliberate misunderstandings, accidental companionship. Never love. Never intimacy. Nothing to dissolve the space between us. We were separated as irrevocably as electrons in an atom, revolving around the nucleus of the nuclear family.

In the face of my parents' wrath, in the isolation of the suburbs, in the powerlessness of childhood, I created an imaginary community — a private island of comfort and warmth and authentic life. Lonely, I dreamed of friendship. Frightened, I dreamed of power. Helpless, I imagined I could heal all wounds. Afraid to fall asleep at night, I rode my spirit-horse — an Appaloosa — from place to place, visiting my imaginary friends. They were squirrels and deer and foxes. They were little girls and old women, with strong hands and deep voices. They were two men, tiny as a thumbprint, who always cried when I moved on. I brought them food and Band-Aids; I ministered to them; I held them tight.

In the next room, my sister lay awake, with her own private dreams and agonies.

I knew that if I ever spoke of my imaginary world, it would fissure and split apart. Just so with the real world; it depended on my silence and duplicity. But how would we maintain the veneer of family? What if we had learned to love each other then? We did not.

This is what family came to mean to me: failure. Failure of nerve: I cowered, did not speak when I needed to, failed to save us. Failure of attention: I forgot, did not look for her, look after her. I failed to find what was precious. Failure of becoming: I did not do what I could, would not bend my back to it.

Now we are both lesbians. As adults, we learned to break through innumerable silences. Slowly, carefully, we learned to love each other. We are bound by blood. We are bound by the dream of lesbian community. But our childhood patterns are restless ghosts that haunt me still.

regret

This is a picture of your great-grandmother, our mother's mother. She was an enormously talented artist who scarcely painted. She drank too much. Her husband beat her up. She suffered from bleak depressions and nervous breakdowns. We were afraid of her as children. She was a good and bad mother to her only child, our mother. And our mother still dwells inside her childhood experience, trying to understand it, trying not to reproduce it, trying to fix it. Mom chose her dreams, her husband and her houseful of children as a kind of conversation with her mother.

In ten years, there were six of us children. Mom was so alone, with her resources so depleted by us. Her patience stretched to the limit; then it was broken, open. She would rage at us, hurt us. This is one of our wounds.

As adults, Wendy and I came to share a gentle companionship with our mother — nothing like the fevered bonding and betrayal we felt as children. Yet still, both of us dwell inside our childhood experience, trying to understand it, trying not to reproduce it, trying to fix it. Wendy became a social worker. She has a hundred friends. She couldn't wait to be a mother. I became an artist. I have few friends. I decided to be childless. We have some things in common, though: We want to heal the world, and we are lesbians.

I see our lives as a kind of conversation with our mother — the mother she was to us. Being women-loving-women is part of this. There was a great lesbian poet called Audre Lorde, who died a month after you were born. She wrote this to her mother, and both Wendy and I understand it sometimes:

… But I have peeled away your anger
down to its core of love
and look mother
I am   a dark temple
where your true spirit rises
beautiful   tough as chestnut …

(*"Black Mother Woman"*)

We peeled away our mother's anger, down to the core of love. It gave us a different chance at living.

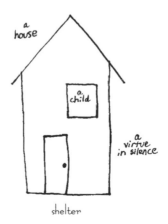

TO SAPPHO, MY SISTER

"Nuclear families" was the name for families like the one we grew up in. The phrase came into the language around 1947, two years after the first nuclear bombs were detonated. The metaphor described our family pretty well, when you add to it the fact that science and society had managed to split the nucleus of the atom, creating a violent explosion.

Families were isolated from one another and then, inside each family, every person was hidden by his or her function. We were lonely and frightened. Sometimes it seemed like all we did was fight. Kids were dependent; there was no escape. Maybe it was just as tough for men and women, but it was all we knew. In all the turmoil of our household, we each seized upon our tiny scrap of power. It was the drama of human relationships inside the nuclear family — everyone going for power over someone else.

Perhaps we became lesbians as a way of escaping that fate, though it didn't begin that way. At least for me, being a lesbian began with a slow-growing love for someone in particular — your aunt Mearnie. In time, I realized it was a political choice to be a woman-loving-woman. There were people who hated and feared us. Wendy and I both worked, in our own ways, to change that. We put aside artwork we wanted to finish, friendships we cherished, and bent our backs to the task at hand. Wendy learned three languages, taught, marched, organized volunteers, raised funds, set up training programs, and co-ordinated care and housing for people with AIDS. I was a publisher and writer. We got so tired of it. Sometimes we were worn to shreds just by the daily things — ugly wisecracks, money problems, a constant low-grade fear of violence.

It was hard being lesbians, so we sought shelter. We tried to fit in, to disappear. Sometimes we contrived an imitation of the nuclear family, since that was the pretence of shelter we knew best. But all those power struggles would rear their heads again: sightless monsters. It was like building a bomb shelter instead of changing the world.

I keep seeking strength by going back to the river, chopping through the ice to remember how I became a lesbian. It was an enormous risk, a leap of faith, the collapse of my identity. It was magic, as I told Mearnie, if that meant a woman's science. It was a fierce desire. I wrote:

the harsh wind of your breathlessness
tears my breath away; my bones
want you. I want you
with the marrow of my bones.

shelter

This is a picture of your great-grandmother, our father's mother. The skin on her hands was transparent, fissured with a thousand hairline cracks. Her index finger was a gnarled claw, twisted with needlework and arthritis. She was many things — among them, shelter. The hundred times I fled to her, mad with youth and enmity, she always kept me from harm. Would you think less of Jesse if I told you about her mad flirtation with her beloved sister's husband? When her sister died, she married him.

Wendy "believes in" family. She asks me: "Who looks after you when you're hurt?"

"Who hurts you?" I counter.

You are my niece, child of my heart — but what is family? Only people as frail as us, and just as splendid. We depend on each other, in particular, and we betray each other — not in abstract categories like lesbian and not, family and not. Sometimes it seems like everyone wants to vanish into categories: sex, sexual identity, family, nation, occupation. They yearn for a sense of belonging, an absolution of sins. They want to feel at home, to be part of something bigger than themselves.

For me, the joy of being lesbian is experiencing the magic of choice, the surprise of desire, the way love invents us. Being lesbian is a struggle against closure, against forgetting, against structuring our psychic past so as to bury it. Belonging is a rare and occasional enchantment; similitude is an oppressive repudiation of human capacity. Family — family that is not the paranoid territory of our childhood — has boundaries that are fluid, meanings that ebb and flow.

Naomi

This is a picture of you taken by your other mother, Claire, when you were nine months old. I keep it on my wall to remind myself to forgo indifference and to dream. My dream for you is not that you will be like us or even that you will like us, though that would bring me pleasure. I dream you will have integrity, like a watershed. I dream you will live always-new, like a river.

Only ten percent of us may be lesbians, but we are all ninety percent water, and water has been my best teacher. Under the ice, and the highways, trapped in giant culverts and beneath our skin —

even when ditched, dyked, diverted and filled with garbage — the water is there, singing its secrets. Our solitude is irrevocable, but we have a kinship with all life, like water. I promise you, as I was never promised: we can be just that delicate, and strong.

Left: Caffyn   Right: Wendy

Barbara Grier and Diane Grier

Interviewed by Andrea L. T. Peterson

Left: Barbara   Right: Donna McBride, Barbara's partner

Left: Geyne Kent, Diane's partner   Right: Diane

Middle-class Values

Barbara and Diane

"I would hate to have a life without sisters," says Diane Grier, younger sister of Naiad Press founder Barbara Grier, and older sister of the happily married Penni Grier. Having a *lesbian* sister is an even greater joy for the elder and the middle Grier. Both concede that their relationship — a very solid friendship with each other and each other's lover — wouldn't be the same if one or the other of them had been heterosexual.

What unique things do lesbian sisters share? According to Diane, there is a closeness between lesbian siblings that is "a step beyond where family can usually get." She likens it to the difference between the comfort and closeness women experience in a room full of other women, and to their caution and self-censorship in "mixed company."

"You must realize," explains Barbara about herself, "that you are dealing with someone who forms all of her affiliations with the belief that lesbians and gay men are really somehow 'other.' They have abilities, passion, strength so superior." Diane is family *and* this mysterious "other." Therefore, "we are family in a sense that is far stronger than family." And, adds Barbara, "a shared sexual orientation gives you the ability to cut through all the Mickey Mouse stuff in families."

The elder two Griers weren't always close. Barbara was born in Cincinnati in 1933 and was a worldly youngster. Mother Grier sat Barbara down at ten years of age and "gave me the entire history of sexuality in the Western Hemisphere, complete with diagrams." A short two years later, Barbara returned from a visit to the library, "having figured out for myself that I was a homosexual, and told my mother. She laughed," Barbara recalls, "and said, 'You're not a homosexual. You're a lesbian because you're a girl.'" Her mother also suggested that Barbara was "a little young," and that perhaps they should "wait six months before telling the newspaper!"

Coming out in the Grier home was not quite the traumatic experience shared by most young gays and lesbians forty years ago. "Mother was raised in New York, in a theatrical family," Diane explains. "Everyone around was artistic," Barbara elaborates. I know now that there were gay men among my mother's friends. I lived in a family that believed all of this kind of thing should be very clearly spelled out ... everything was discussed. Being homosexual was not queer or weird. It was part of the landscape."

That philosophy, coupled with the path Barbara had already forged, made Diane's coming out a few years later that much the easier. "I don't remember not being gay," says Diane. There isn't a precise moment of enlightenment Diane can point to, but she had no doubts: "I never gave a passing thought to men."

Reflecting on the story about a girl who claimed that, in her bassinet in the maternity ward, she turned and looked at the little baby girl in the next bassinet and "knew," Diane says she's been a lesbian "forever." Her mother faced a real challenge trying to "teach the facts of life to Diane. She just wasn't interested," Barbara recounts.

"Barbara probably knew about me before I did," says Diane. Not so, according to Barbara, who left home when she was eighteen and Diane was twelve, and claims she didn't know about her sister's sexual orientation until Diane was in her late teens. She doesn't remember who told her about Diane, or when exactly she found out. "To my knowledge," Barbara emphasizes, "Diane didn't know about herself when I left home." And, although she "wasn't surprised" to find out that Diane was a lesbian, Barbara insists that she "had no prior inkling. But," Barbara is quick to add, "I am probably the second or third most self-centred being on the planet."

Barbara and Diane have achieved a closeness that is remarkable, considering the fact that they really did have radically different childhood experiences. "Barbara," says Diane, "was born old. She was never a kid. I got to know my sister as an adult."

In fact, Barbara did practically raise both of her younger sisters during their earliest years. Then, when Barbara was fourteen, her parents divorced, and the children were separated for a time. Barbara lived with her father, and the two younger girls were sent to a Catholic boarding school for a few months. Says Barbara, "They were more vulnerable to the turmoil. Diane and Pennie weren't abused, but they were terrified."

Just a few years after the family had broken up, eighteen-year-old Barbara set out to make her own life. The younger girls, just twelve and eight at the time, were still years away from their own independence. Around the time that Diane was trying to come out, Barbara's wanderings came to rest in her first long-term relationship (it lasted twenty years). "I was busy," explains Barbara, "building up the centre of the universe in which I would carefully sit." That relationship took her out of circulation for two decades.

During that time, Diane was more intimate with her younger sister, Penni — they were a little closer in age and a lot closer geographically. Diane also eventually left home, found and fell in love with Geyne, her first — and only — love, and began a relationship that has lasted for more than thirty years.

Those two decades, during which Diane and Barbara lived in their own worlds and had little contact with each other, were important ones for both sisters. Diane forged her career and her relationship; Barbara sequestered herself with her companion, Helen Bennett, a preacher's daughter.

Helen Bennett was seeking to undo a lifetime of violated privacy, having spent her years before Barbara living in the fishbowl that is a preacher's family's life. She wanted to be as far away "from the human race as possible." Consequently, Barbara and Helen had minimal contact with family, and even less contact with the rest of the outside world. Difficult though it is to imagine the Barbara Grier of the '90s cloistered away somewhere, such was the case. And, she says, "it was very fortuitous." Those years gave her the time and opportunity to collect what is reputed to be the largest gay and lesbian book collection in the world, to write for *The Ladder*, to work non-stop for the movement, and to lay the groundwork for her future very out, very active lesbian life as one of the founders of Naiad and a spokesperson for the lesbian community. "I had twenty very happy years with Helen," Barbara reflects. "There are aspects of that life that I can't have in this one. That was the romantic non-reality Helen and I lived in."

There is also much in Barbara's present-day life that she couldn't have in that previous one. In fact, it wasn't until 1972, when Barbara began her relationship with her current partner, Donna McBride, that Barbara and Diane developed a relationship with each other, and with their respective partners.

Barbara explains that, unlike Helen, "Donna is very family oriented." After meeting Donna, Barbara renewed her connection with both of her sisters, and her relationship with Diane, with whom she had the most in common, was able to flourish.

Speaking of their relationship, both sisters agree that they're "the best of friends." But that friendship got off to a slow start. The dynamic between the sisters had to change — from that of parent and child, to a friendship between equals. The transition wasn't easy. There was "a really rocky time," says Diane, reflecting on her eventual realization of just how important her sister was to her. Now, Diane considers Barbara and herself to be sisters first, but also very good friends. "Barbara," she suspects, "would probably say it the other way."

Indeed, Barbara would and does. She says that she and Diane are friends first — good friends. This difference in perception may come from Barbara's formative early role as pseudo-parent to Diane, not to any inequity in the friendship. Indeed, it is clear that the two women really do have a solid, positive friendship — a friendship they share with each other's partners as well.

The sisters also share many similarities. "It is a matter of degrees," asserts Diane. Barbara says of Diane and Diane's partner, Geyne, "they are active politically. Not like we are, but they probably have a wider circle of personal friends than we do." Indeed, Diane and Geyne have a vast network of lesbian friends, while Barbara and Donna know many women but are truly good friends with only a few couples — including Diane and Geyne.

"Diane and Geyne are literate and bright," says Barbara. "I'm a real snob about that. They are conscious, reading, politically aware, savvy people." She doesn't add, "like we are," but it's implied. Barbara and Donna are more involved than Diane and Geyne in the broader political scene, and they are clearly more vocal and more visible. There was a time, though, when Diane and Geyne were more visible in the lesbian community — before they retired and moved out of the Kansas City area, where so many of their friends live. "When we were younger," says Diane, "and earning good money, we were more involved. We wrote more cheques than picked up placards," but involvement and commitment are still involvement and commitment. They were often instrumental in fund raising and doing work for women musicians like Holly Near.

Surprisingly, Barbara is, according to Diane, "more conservative." Not surprisingly, both sisters agree that Barbara is the more aggressive personality — maybe even a little imposing. But Diane insists that she, too, is also "very assertive, aggressive ... in business." In fact, she says, that has often landed her in trouble.

Both sisters enjoy sports, good food and beer, says Barbara, "and we share some other wonderful secret things ... paper fetishes, a leftover from growing up poor. We are both immaculate. Our houses look like they have been prepped for surgery!"

Both sisters also agree that, were they not lesbians, their relationship would be different. Barbara doesn't tolerate heterosexual company too well; Diane doesn't share the aversion, as her relationship with her younger sister, Penni, indicates.

"No," says Barbara emphatically, she and Diane would not be as close as they are if Diane were heterosexual. "I am sure," she adds, "I like her better because she's a dyke.That is where my affinity really is ... that's the place where I am who I am. It is who I am. It informs who I am and how I look at the world, how I look at my sister Diane ... and my sister Penni." While Barbara likes her brother-in-law well enough, and she and her youngest sister certainly get along fine, they really aren't good friends.

A striking similarity among the three Grier sisters is that they have all found stable, lasting relationships. Did they learn to embrace monogamy in their childhood home? Although their mother and father divorced, the story doesn't end there. In their old age, mother and father again married each other.

Barbara, by her own admission, had "slept with every available female" by the time she was seventeen. "I am really a sexual being," she adds, in an effort to explain the pre-monogamy exploits. It is a part of her that she believes some people might find surprising. When she found love at seventeen, though, she settled into a loving monogamous relationship for two decades. After that relationship ended, she began her current one, which is now pushing twenty-five years.

Diane met and "married" her first love thirty-two years ago. They continue to enrich each other's lives today. Youngest sister Penni met and married her first love more than twenty years ago. She and her husband are still together, raising the only Grier grandchild.

"Maybe it [the tendency toward monogamy] is familial," Barbara muses. It never occurred to her to "be in anything but a permanent relationship ... to fall in love forever. We're really kind of ordinary," says Barbara, "so middle class and so middle western." A similar permanency informs the relationship between Barbara and Diane. In spite of the differences in their life experiences, in spite of the differences in their personalities and in spite of the geographical distance between them, their friendship is vital to the lives of both.

Diane asserts with absolute certainty that "my life would be diminished if Barbara were suddenly not in it. I think it would crush me. She's been very, very good to me, there for me, my whole life."

Barbara is even more precise about just how the relationship has an impact on her life. "Diane," she says, "is my only remaining connection to my family in any real sense. I would probably forget I ever had a family without Diane. She truly is family in a sense that is stronger than family."

Barbara

Diane

Catherine Hughes and Mikaela Hughes

Left: Catherine   Right: Mikaela

The Hughes Family Chronicles

Catherine

This past spring, I drove with my parents from their home in Kingston, Ontario, to New York City, to attend my brother Daniel's graduation from the Graduate School of the New York Academy of Art. During that drive, I heard the detailed account of what was happening in my parents' lives in the months before and after my conception.

The setting is Johannesburg, South Africa, in 1964, which was the year Nelson Mandela and other leaders of the anti-apartheid struggle were tried and convicted of treason and sentenced to life in prison. My parents are both white and they grew up in South Africa. That year, my mother, Margaret, turned twenty-seven and my father, Ian, was thirty. They were totally against apartheid. Ian was a university lecturer and Margaret was teaching art at the Johannesburg School of Art. They had met through the Catholic Church where they had become friends and then lovers. The first time they had intercourse, Margaret became pregnant. Not long afterwards, they married and Margaret had to quit her job because married women were not allowed to teach at her school.

Following this, a further series of events occurred which led to my parents' decision to leave South Africa.

Ian and his father, Viv, were questioned by the security police after several members of the family, including Ian and Margaret, and a friend, Tod (who is black), spent a weekend at a guesthouse run by nuns. Their obvious friendship aroused suspicions by the authorities since the guesthouse happened to be on the main escape route for politicals trying to leave South Africa. Luckily, neither Tod nor Margaret was questioned, Tod because Ian told the security police that Tod had "one of those unpronounceable African names" and said that he didn't know where Tod lived (they lived together at the time), and Margaret because she had contracted the measles. The doctor thought Margaret had German measles and advised her to have an abortion. It turned out that she had regular measles and she carried me to term. During this period of a few months, a bomb exploded on the "whites only" platform at the train station in Johannesburg. Ian and Margaret knew two of the people who were picked up by the police and detained without charges in connection with the bombing. Ian wrote a letter to the paper, saying that the people who had been arrested should either be charged or released; shortly after the letter was published, he received a death threat in the mail.

While all this was happening in South Africa, Gilbert, a friend of Ian's and fellow South African mathematician who was living in the United States, urged Ian and Margaret to move there. In the end, my parents decided to emigrate and Gilbert found Ian a job teaching at Fairleigh Dickinson University in New Jersey. They left South Africa in October 1964 and I was born in Summit, New Jersey, on February 24, 1965. Perhaps the events leading up to my birth partly explain my serious character!

By the time Mikaela came along, we were living in Manhattan, where we stayed for a year. Then we moved again to Pennsylvania, and then on to Kingston, Ontario, where my brother, Daniel, was born. While the three of us were growing up, our household usually included more people than our nuclear family. For a while we lived with my best friend, Samantha, and her parents. There was usually at least one student from the university living with us and, later on, three of Mikaela's and my friends spent a year living in our house. There were also friends who came and cooked meals, ate with us and dropped in for tea and talk — lots of talk. Even now, it's hard to sit in my parents' kitchen for fifteen minutes and not become involved in a big discussion about some personal or political issue.

When I was little, I spent a lot of time listening to these conversations until I had enough confidence to participate. Sometimes, Waffle meetings were held at our house. (The Waffle was a left-wing caucus of Canada's New Democratic Party. It's official name was The Movement for an Independent Socialist Canada. It split from the party during the time that meetings were held in our house.) Everyone wore sweaters and shawls because the largest room, where the meetings were held, was also the coldest. I loved to sit quietly among these people who held such strong beliefs. I doubt I understood much of what was said, but I felt I was being included in something important. All the talk in our family — about equality, women's liberation, the anti-apartheid struggle, Marxism, Vietnam, the peace movement, colonialism, et cetera — was a great base from which I developed strong values and learned how to stand up for, and express, my beliefs.

Ian has taught me by his example, and he keeps reminding me with his questions, to be precise in my political analysis and to stand back and look at the big picture. Ever since I was a child, Margaret has encouraged my creative expression and resourcefulness. She has helped me to see the complexity of life and to have confidence in my own judgment. What I have learned from my parents has helped me to understand events in the world and given me the strange notion that people with egalitarian ideals can have an effect on those events. It has helped me to become active around queer rights and to see how fighting for those rights is part of a much larger struggle. It has also helped me to express my feelings and ideas through artwork.

Both my parents always supported my choices and encouraged me to fulfil my dreams despite the obstacles created by sexism. My girlfriends and I had dreams of farming together — and although I replaced those dreams with other ones for years, here I am now, making my living by farming and producing Jersey milk with my compañera, Jane Morrigan.

Even though so much was shared with us children in discussions, I don't remember much talk about sexuality, and I was quite shy about my sexual feelings as a teenager. I didn't tell anybody about the fun I had masturbating nor about my emotional and sexual feelings for other girls. An early experience which made me aware of my lesbian feelings and introduced me to homophobia happened when I went on a camping trip with the girls' outdoor club in high school. Three of my friends were on the trip, but they must have been closer to one another than they were to me because, when we were told we could have three people to a tent, I was the one left out. I shared a tent with two other girls whom I didn't know as well. The first night, I made up the sleeping bags so that one of the other girls and I would sleep together, because it was so cold. We had agreed to do this. That night, we heard the girls in the other tent laughing and carrying on and I guessed they were playing sex games with each other. The next day one of them told me that she'd heard it was perfectly natural for girls to go through a phase of having sexual attractions for each other between the ages of fourteen and sixteen. She didn't refer to what they'd been doing the night before. I wished I had been invited to their tent!

The next night, the girl with whom I'd shared sleeping bags made them up before I got to the tent, and she made them up separately. It was the first homophobic reaction I had felt directed toward me. I don't think I knew the word *homophobia*, but I understood what was happening.

The next year I became involved with a few guys, but I was much closer to one of the young women living in our house. I would have loved it if our relationship had become sexual. I wanted to take off with her on adventures. Then, in art college, I fell madly in love with one of my special women friends. For one long night, we lay in her bed together and neither of us could sleep because of the sexual tension. Later that day we went for coffee and she asked me why I hadn't been able to sleep. I said I didn't know! Finally, a few weeks later, I stood outside her door for half an hour before I had the courage to go in and tell her I was attracted to her. She said she was very attracted to me, too, but that she couldn't be a lesbian because she couldn't handle dealing with homophobia, especially her father's homophobia.

She ignored me and avoided me for most of the next two weeks. This hurt me deeply. She thought I was pressuring her to get involved with me, but I was much too scared of losing her friendship to even think of it. She and I did manage to restore our friendship eventually, but in the meantime I felt miserable. I was learning about the power that homophobia has to drive a wedge between people who love each other.

I was still hurting when I went to visit my family in Kingston a few weeks later. When I arrived home, Margaret noticed how much time I was spending staring into space. One day, she, Mikaela and I went to the cottage my family shares with my old friend Samantha and her family. Margaret and I were standing looking out over the beautiful water when she said she had something she wanted to tell me. She explained that she had had a lesbian relationship when I was ten, with a woman I had known as a close family friend.

I was amazed that they had been lovers. Ian had full knowledge of the situation, but I hadn't picked up on it at all. I just remembered that this woman related to me in a very open way and made me feel that my experience and opinions counted.

When Margaret told me all this, I thought it was great that she had been free enough to become involved with another woman. I was very curious about their relationship. I also thought that this would be a good time to tell Margaret about my feelings for the woman I was in love with. I told her about my troubles, and then we walked up the hill to the cottage to join Mikaela. As we walked, Margaret asked me if I thought she should tell Mikaela about her lesbian relationship. I said, "Yes," with an "of course" sort of tone in my voice. So, Margaret took a deep breath and told Mikaela the skeleton of the story she had told me. Mikaela said "So what?" and Margaret left it at that.

Where does Daniel fit into this story? Margaret didn't tell him about her lesbian relationship at the same time as she told Mikaela and me. When he came to visit Jane and me, five or six years later, he told us that he'd known about it for quite a while because one of the sons of the woman who had been Margaret's lover was a good friend of his. Dan had found out from him. He was hurt that Margaret hadn't talked to him. He was also hurt that Mikaela and I hadn't talked to him about being lesbians. Previously, I had thought he felt that Mik and I, as lesbians, rejected all men — and therefore him. Apparently, though, what bothered him was that we had left him out of an important part of our lives. Ever since that visit, Dan and I have shared more of our intimate feelings. When we talk, it is great for me, because Daniel has an openness and an ease in expressing himself, which influences me positively.

As the two dyke sisters in this unconventional family, Mikaela and I are quite similar in some ways. We have both been outspoken about our beliefs and we sometimes have difficulty expressing our most intimate feelings. Neither of us, however, can hide our feelings, because they show on our faces.

Of course, Mikaela and I have our own distinct personalities. I am resourceful, independent, stubborn and I tend to go overboard with my feelings of responsibility, but I also have a wild side that would like to express itself more often. It sometimes comes out in my artwork but I don't make enough time for art. Margaret's latest advice to me is to be selfish and take the time I need. Mikaela is very committed to her beliefs and her work. She is creative and meticulous in all her endeavours. She is also affectionate, generous and loving. She spends more time reflecting on the humorous side of life than I do and she is mischievous. As a child, she would play with Dan's and my emotions. For example, when we had chocolate, she would eat hers slowly and watch Dan and me drool over it after we had gobbled ours down. She always gave us some in the end. She was so kind. I guess I didn't pay much attention to the vicious fights she and Dan had.

Now that Mikaela and I are both out dykes, we have some obvious common interests. We met up last year at the Gay, Lesbian and Bisexual Games and the twenty-fifth anniversary of the Stonewall riot in New York City. Jane and I got to meet Mikaela's teammates on her dyke soccer team, the South London Studs. Our friend, Joy, who used to be Mik's lover and is still my "sister outlaw" (Mikaela coined this term), came down from Kingston, Ontario, to march with us too. I think Mik and I would still be close if either one of us was heterosexual because we're pretty open-minded and we love each other. However, we might not feel quite as at home with each other inside dyke culture.

As Mikaela and I came out more and more, our family began to talk more openly about lesbianism, problems in lesbian communities and the politics of the queer liberation movement. These topics got integrated into the usual discussions that happen at the Hughes kitchen table. Ian and Margaret have participated in Gay, Lesbian and Bisexual Pride marches, and Margaret is one of the few members of the Kingston Parents and Friends of Lesbians and Gays. Daniel defends queers passionately when he hears us being put down.

As well, Mikaela's and my lovers have been welcomed into the family. The first time Jane and I visited Ian and Margaret, we drove from Nova Scotia and arrived in Kingston fairly late one evening. We had a little visit and went to bed, tired from the drive. In the morning, when Jane and I were still in bed, Ian came in, lay down between us and started asking Jane about the dairy industry in Nova Scotia! Since then, Margaret and Ian have visited us many times. Ian has worked on mathematics problems at our home and read books in his special chair on the hill. Although he once said of lesbian rights, "It's not my issue," the last time he was here he read most of the lesbian anthologies Margaret had given Jane and me.

Margaret keeps leaving us more reminders of her love and support by taking on carpentry and other projects for us, and giving us beautiful pieces of her pottery. She's always dying to help us out financially, too, but I'm impossibly independent and Jane's the same. Margaret asks me if I'll please accept some money, Ian tells her to let me ask if I need help and I tell Ian to leave Margaret alone. We go around in circles like that.

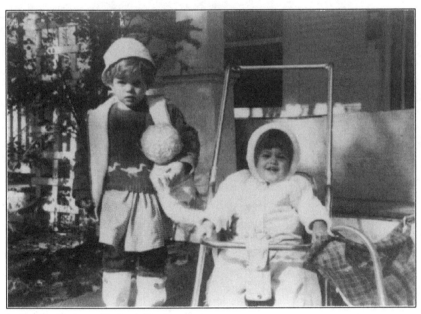

Left: Catherine   Right: Mikaela

Mikaela

From the moment she was born, Catherine faced the world with energy and interest. Her cry as she entered the world was brief, perhaps because she was quite ready to leave her protective womb and begin to explore wider boundaries. Lying on Margaret's stomach, she surveyed this new and strange world around her. Her first words all had to do with activity — verbs in the present participle: *running, jumping*. Her first sentence — "Baby, aw'byself, trundle on" — reflected both her independent nature and her unique fashion sense. She was fond of a particular baby attire known as a "trundle bundle." Summit, New Jersey, was the place of her birth — an appropriate place, since the little Catherine would climb everything, even the curtains. By the time I arrived, a year and a half later, she was already scaling the monkey bars in Tompkins Square, in New York City.

Our parents, concerned over the possibility of their first-born succumbing to sibling rivalry over the new baby, were careful when bringing me home to Catherine. Ian carried me, while Margaret went ahead to greet Catherine, who was staying with my "mother-god," Terry. Far from being jealous, my older sister rushed out to meet me, pushing aside our mother and crying: "Baby, baby, baby!" We've been friends ever since, so the story goes.

I have the unique honour in our family of being the only child to have been conceived and born in the same city — the same country, even — and I also had the easiest entry into the world. I was Margaret's least-painful delivery and I was crying as I emerged, not quite sure whether I wanted to leave my comfortable home. Once here, however, I was quite content — a happy, brown baby, small, compact and cuddly. I enjoyed my lot in life, whether I was being passed from lap to lap or set down in the rhubarb patch to fend for myself among the giant leaves.

I was two years and nineteen days old when Daniel entered our lives. That was the year I decided to stop wearing dresses. We had left Pennsylvania two months previously to move to Ontario. With the chaos of our lives swirling around me as furniture and clothing were packed into vans, I had sat calmly on my tricycle, kissing the boy next door — the last boy I ever kissed.

I was not quite sure about the new baby brother. After about a year, he was getting into my toys and being a nuisance in my life. I reacted by crawling around on all fours pretending to be a cat and meowing pitifully. Catherine was more interested in him and wanted to pick him up. I can imagine what it must have been like for the little Daniel, entering a family in which he was the youngest, the littlest and the only boy. With two older siblings already well established, it was difficult to find the undivided attention that he wanted. He discovered that, by making a scene, he would get it. This infuriated me, but Catherine was somehow too mature to be disturbed by him.

On the other hand, there was little competition between Catherine and me because we had different interests and friends. I also thought that Catherine was simply above the pettiness of jealousy. I would torment her, though. Standing in my highchair and pointing at her, I would cry: "You Mikaela! Me Catherine!" and laugh. Incensed, she would try to defend herself, but that only made the joke funnier, for what kind of defence is there against someone who is lying and knows it? It was only later that I thought: "What is so wrong with being Mikaela? I've lived with it all my life." I guess I was stealing her identity, and someone as independent as Catherine would not stand for that. Later, she told me that she would have preferred to have been called "Mikaela" or to have had a more unusual name of her own. "Catherine" was such a common name in Anglo North

America, although it had not been quite so normal when we were living in Kenya. Ironically, it was her eyes that I wished I could have. In our dark-eyed, dark-haired family, her blue eyes were somehow exotic. I was unaware that, in our small Ontario city, blue eyes were very common. Coincidentally, perhaps, all my partners have had blue eyes. It is interesting that the things both of us wished for that the other possessed were things that we felt would make us different and special.

In my kindergarten class, I tended to play with the boys. One day, our teacher asked us to form two lines, with girls in one and boys in the other. As I found my appropriate place, my friends cried out: "But Mikaela's a boy!" Somehow I had become a tomboy by default. I used to refer to that part of my childhood as "when I was a boy."

A poem I wrote after my best friend Andrew had moved to Australia and my cat Stephanie had died described the differences between my outer and inner worlds at that time:

I seem to be a boy
But really I'm a girl.
I seem to be happy
But really I am sad.
I seem to not have a cat
But really I have a cat that is dead.

The childhood issues that exist in this poem — the differences between how I feel about myself and how I feel society views me; the balance of pain and elation; and the changing relationships with friends, family and lovers — are quite potent even in my life today.

Our mother made a special effort to show that Catherine and I, as women, could be whatever we wanted to be. For me, this meant that it was fine to be a tomboy. For Catherine, it meant that she was able to do what she wanted without feeling restricted. Her friends were all girls and they would go downhill skiing and white-water canoeing, or they would go camping and get caught on cliffs. She would climb trees all the way to the top, while I stood at the bottom, not even attempting the lowest branch. Yet, somehow, she was not a tomboy and I was. Later, as a young teenager, I decided that there was a contradiction between being a feminist and a tomboy. As a tomboy, I wanted to be a boy; yet that indicated there was something wrong with being a girl, which didn't seem quite right.

Margaret was "the best mom in the world. That is what me and Catherine think," I wrote in another poem when I was six. While I knew that this was true, I thought that every child must feel this way about her mother. It was only later in life that I discovered that not all mothers offered the acceptance, encouragement, selflessness and unconditional love I found with Margaret, or possessed the intelligence, creativity and strength of character to be a positive role model — a self-employed potter with "tow hundred killergrams of clay."

Ian was, and is, less demonstrative than Margaret. In their thirty years of marriage, Margaret has never seen him cry. The two of us share a silly sense of humour — as does Daniel, though Daniel has taken it almost to the height of stand-up comedy. I feel that I am similar to Ian in many other ways: I am eccentric, laid back and not very emotionally expressive. When I was in school, I was shocked to discover that Ian (as well as Margaret) worried about me.

At the age of eleven, I returned to Ontario with my family after spending two years in Kenya. I found the majority of children at school to be very cold, uninterested in others, and often cruel to kids who were perceived as different. At the time I couldn't see why particular kids were chosen to be the brunt of malicious teasing. There seemed to be a history and rules that I didn't understand. Whereas in Nairobi I had been the leader of a gang of boys at school and had always had both female and male friends, in Canada I felt that there were numerous unspoken rules around gender. Girls played with girls, boys with boys. Girls played girl games. Boys played boy games. I had no close male friends throughout high school, and even university. Boys had turned from potential friends into potential boyfriends. Since I wasn't interested in boyfriends, I had little or nothing to do with them. Ontario had become a foreign world to me. To top it off, I had returned from Africa with a funny accent, which I lost as quickly as possible.

Catherine also found it difficult to fit in, not so much because of gender issues but because we didn't watch *Dallas* on television and we didn't share the values of the majority of our schoolmates. Even Daniel felt that he was an outsider, but his reaction was different. He would have preferred that our family try to fit in by changing rather than by being accepted for who we are. He wanted wall-to-wall carpets. He wanted Margaret to be dainty and cook chicken for supper. He said that if we lived in suburbia he would keep his bedroom clean.

It was when I was in high school that I became aware of the existence of lesbians for the first time. When I was sixteen, a friend of mine told me she was a lesbian. I remember saying that I couldn't imagine myself kissing another woman. The funny thing is, I couldn't imagine kissing a man either. Sure, I had the occasional crush — on the captain of my hockey team, on a Polish boy when we went back to Kenya — but somehow they weren't sexual.

I never masturbated, nor did I have sexual fantasies, though I was well aware that they existed. Maybe I had read too much Jane Austen and Lucy Maud Montgomery and was waiting for the perfect ... the perfect what? At first it was a member of the opposite sex, but when I realized that there were other options I revised it to just "someone." In a way, I felt myself to be asexual. Many of our friends identified themselves as straight, bisexual or gay. I said simply, "I'm not." Even Catherine was trying out boyfriends. Though Catherine and I never talked to each other about our sexuality or emotions at that time, I assumed that my sexual orientation, whatever it was, would be fine with her.

It wasn't until I was in university that I fell in love. This was it! It was right out of the romantic novels I'd read, except that our genders were the same. There was something special about a lesbian relationship. It required sacrifice. It went against the grain — all for the sake of love. To me this made it more precious.

Coming out to Margaret was simple — almost mandatory — as soon as I realized what was going on. Catherine had come out to her, and vice versa, earlier the same summer, and they had come out to me. At the time I said little and felt uncomfortable that it was being made into such a serious issue. I felt that I should contribute to the conversation, so I added that I had never even kissed anyone, male or female. I had not expected either Catherine's or Margaret's coming out, but I was not shocked. I had simply learned something new about two people I loved dearly.

The only difficult thing about coming out to Margaret was my complete lack of appropriate language. I wanted her to know about my newfound sexuality immediately, but I didn't know how to communicate it. I was unaccustomed to verbalizing my emotions and was painfully shy about discussing my sexuality. I walked into the kitchen and said in a very matter-of-fact tone, "I am having an affair with Rooth," in much the same way as I would have said, "We're out of toilet paper." I wasn't asking for support, because I knew it was already there. I wasn't asking for anything. I just wanted her to know — just as I have wanted her to know about other important things in my life.

Margaret, being herself, said some words of reassurance but knew I didn't want to talk about it; she then reminded me that we had to put some oil on the pesto she was preparing or it would go brown. I never told Ian or Daniel directly, since I knew Margaret was much better at discussing these things than I.

I am glad that I have learnt a language for emotions and for sex. Sometimes I still find it difficult to be open about my sexuality with certain straight people, even when I really want to be. I don't know whether this is internalized homophobia, fear of their reaction or simply shyness. It seems to me that Catherine is able to be more open, more out, than me. I admire her for it and sometimes wish I was more like her in this. I am learning, just as I am learning to verbalize my emotions.

At times, when I learn of the difficult childhoods of many of my friends, I feel myself lucky simply to have parents who didn't beat me, molest me or make me feel worthless. It's sad that I consider myself lucky to have had something that should be the fundamental right of every child. When I tell my lesbian and gay friends about our parents — about how accepting and supportive they are and have been — many tell me how lucky I am and describe the frustrations that they have had with their own families because of their sexual orientation. Some have never come out to their parents because they are justifiably scared of violence or rejection. Many see their biological families infrequently and keep them at arm's length. Other parents continue to care for their children but refuse to acknowledge that they are lesbian or gay, and ignore their friends and lovers. As the majority of my lesbian and gay friends are out, this rejection of an important aspect of their identity can be very painful.

Ironically, in a family that celebrates our differences, it is Daniel, the straight, white male — the "normal" one — who feels that somehow he was left out. Though he feels more appreciated now, and more a part of the family, as a child he would often say that he was adopted. Because there were few boys among our close family friends, Daniel would frequently find himself with three or four older girls. Often, the other girls were Catherine's age and were her friends. While I was usually happy to do my own thing or tag along quietly in this type of situation, Daniel was more aggressive and wanted to be the centre of attention. This would lead to fights, particularly with me, which I hated.

When I was feeling particularly exasperated with him, Margaret would tell me that she and her younger brother used to fight but eventually became friends. I knew better: Daniel and I would never get along with each other. How could I ever have respect for someone who took my stuff, who believed he would have his action men for the rest of his life, who wasted his money on hockey cards rather than something decent like comic books and who thought the Bee Gees were better than the Beatles? By the time Daniel was financing trips to Toronto with his 1979 Wayne Gretzky cards, our old animosities had disappeared and I had begun to truly appreciate his sense of humour.

I also appreciate Daniel's support. It took a while for him to feel comfortable enough to tell his friends that we were lesbians, but now he says he's proud of us and tells everyone. Apart from the fact that Daniel is my brother, a wonderful person and I love him dearly, he is also an important ally. Because he is a man and straight, he can influence many of his friends who might never listen to us lesbians.

I ask myself how it would have been different if Catherine were straight. Would it have been easier or more difficult? Would we have been closer or farther apart? In some ways I feel that it wouldn't have made much difference since I know that my lesbianism would have been accepted by her and our family, regardless of her own orientation. Some of the details, such as coming out, would have been more difficult because I would have had to talk more to the rest of the family about my sexuality. I would have had no one to do the dirty work for me.

I think that, as lesbians, Catherine and I share a certain understanding and common experience which require no words. At the same time, we make assumptions about each other that are not necessarily true, and our misconceptions might be exposed more easily if we were less similar and had to talk more in order to understand each other. Regardless, it's nice to have an ally.

These days, it is only infrequently that our whole family is together at once. Whenever we do meet, however, you can be sure there will be lots of food — the Hughes feeding frenzy — lots of discussion, lots of bickering and lots of love. Somehow, even though our geographical distance varies, we seem to just get closer and closer.

Carol Camper
and Diana Andrews

Carol

Diana

Something in
Common

Carol

My lesbian sister, Diana, and I were not raised together. Our mother had several children at a very young age and the older ones were fostered or adopted. I was adopted, whereas Diana was kept and raised by our mother. We did not meet until I was nearly eighteen and she was almost thirteen. When we did met, I found out that Diana and I had things in common: we both enjoyed athletics, although she took her interest much farther than I ever did; Diana enjoys foreign languages and pursued a degree in French, and I excelled in languages in high school. Though we have things in common that might "run in the family," Diana and I are also very different people, especially where temperament, politics and outlook are concerned. I was not around when she was little, so we have been "unknown factors" in each other's lives. Diana was the big sister in her family until I and our oldest sister returned to the fold. It must have been quite an adjustment for her to make.

I now realize that I was attracted to women from a very young age. In fact, my first crush was on the beautiful mother of one of my kindergarten classmates. I remember her jet black hair, creamy complexion and stiletto heels. She had an air about her of mystery and sadness. Ever since, I have been a fan of Elizabeth Taylor — I think Liz reminded me of her. I had crushes on girls in high school, but the heterosexual imperative was so intense that I could not fully recognize this. Because I also had crushes on guys, I thought I was like everybody else. Whatever fear or questioning I had about my feelings for girls was soothed by my liberal reading material, which indicated that homosexual feelings (ones that would pass) were a normal part of heterosexuality. Before I had a chance to ask the question, it was already answered. I did have a few petting sessions with another girl in my school, but I did not discuss or speculate upon these experiences. They were simply put away somewhere in my head, where they would not intrude upon my real life (until the next time it happened).

In many ways, I was fortunate to find the husband that I did, in that he felt "safe" and was very understanding (which was important to me, an eighteen-year-old incest survivor). I told him of my interest in other women very early on in our relationship. He was the first person I ever told. He was totally non-judgmental about it through the years. In retrospect, I would bet he never took my feelings seriously. He could indulge me because he assumed there was no threat to my need for him. My emerging lesbianism was only one of several reasons why we broke up after fifteen years of marriage.

I say that I'm a lesbian because I like women, not because I don't like men. People who know I am an incest survivor used to speculate that it was my pain that drove me into the arms of women. It is true that there were times when it drove me out of the arms of men, but it was my own desire that brought me to women. I had some good sexual experiences with men, but eventually I could no longer sustain enough interest in them; I was not interested in returning lovemaking. Toward the end of my marriage, I had probably become a "do-me queen." I don't think my husband objected to this (although I wasn't letting him "do me" enough), but I knew it wasn't fair to him that I would rarely return any favours.

I always say that I was "out" a year before I had sex with a woman. This is because I was in therapy and had become able to fully see and articulate my desires for women. The next step was to find one. I attended a lesbian discussion group at the University of Toronto, and through this group I met a woman who knew I was looking for my first time. She kindly offered. I took her up on her offer and it was wonderful. I felt like I had come home for the first time. I am now in a long-term relationship.

When I came out to my youngest sister, she told me about Diana. I was surprised, and yet not surprised, at the same time. A number of things fell into place — for example, the fact that I had almost always seen her with women. We had not been close, so it wasn't strange that I didn't know much about Diana. I knew that eventually we would see each other in the lesbian community, so I decided that I would let her run into me in one of these spaces and find out this way. I thought she would be very surprised because she had known me as a long-married woman. Eventually we did meet at a Toronto lesbian bar, and Diana was indeed surprised. I'm not sure she believed me when I said I was there for the same reason as she. She made some comment indicating that she thought I might be there for sociological reasons (I assumed she meant "field work"), since I worked in the social-services field.

I enjoy having a lesbian sister. We have had fun going to bars and dances together and keeping each other company in what are sometimes stressful environments. We also have a gay brother but have little contact with him. It's interesting that, out of eight children, three of us are gay. The three of us were raised entirely apart, so it's clear to me that our homosexuality is not due to any aspect of our upbringing.

Since I am completely estranged from my adoptive family (and my adoptive mother is dead), I appreciate the contact with my natural family. As a child, my existence was very isolated and filled with abuse and neglect. It was of great value to me to find my "real" family. I have not received any negative feedback from them about being a lesbian, although my mother once said she thought it was a "phase" that people are supposed to grow out of after adolescence. Getting to know one another is a process that continues. The squabbles, disagreements and other general conflicts I have had with some of my siblings (the sisters usually — there are four of us in total) eventually made me realize that I do have a family (even though I am a latecomer to it), since families do fight. I don't think our temperaments will change, but Diana and I do seem to be more similar now in our politics and outlook. Out of my whole family, it is Diana and our youngest sister to whom I am closest. I know there is potential for even more closeness, and that is something I would like.

Diana

I was born in Toronto on September 30, 1960, and was the oldest girl of the four children my mother raised. My lesbian sister, Carol, and I were not raised together. It was by coincidence that Carol discovered she was related to me. She had been adopted at birth and first came into my life when I was in my teens, under the pretence of being a visiting "family friend."

For the better part of my life, I was raised as a single-parent child, along with my older brother, my younger (by eleven months) brother and my younger (by four years) sister. It would not be fair to say that I was neglected or abused, in the clinical sense of the word, but my upbringing included dysfunction and deceit. My mother was very inconsistent in her mothering. Her moods would often swing from mild depression to indifference, to anger. For the most part, I, as the oldest girl, was in charge of the household when she was not home.

This was very frustrating, as I felt powerless to enforce rules that also applied to my older brother. He systematically, and with mocking sarcasm, ignored anything that issued from my mouth on behalf of my mother, who was habitually out with friends and socializing in her "entertainer manqué" mode. My father was "unceremoniously asked to leave" when I was ten, and a new person emerged immediately to replace him. I didn't understand why my father had to leave, and the presence of this new person created tension between my mother and me which increased over the years as my cumulative responsibilities and her expectations increased, often without the accompanying moral and emotional supports.

As a result of this, I grew up to be very independent, somewhat opinionated, strong-willed and passionate about fairness and fair play. Carol and I are opposites in our personalities, especially the way we express our emotions. She is reserved, reflective, controlled and protective; I am direct, expressive, animated and uncompromising.

Like many lesbians, when I look back at my childhood, I can now see the "signs and symptoms" of lesbianism. I was very athletic, assertive and decisive, always supported the underdog, and liked control whenever the opportunity presented itself. I also had little crushes on my neighbourhood friends, especially if they were feminine and yielding. I played "house" a lot and always wanted to be "the father" because he was in control and had so much freedom to do as he pleased — within reason, of course.

My tomboyishness was never questioned (by myself or others) because physically I was girlish (although strong) and my face was feminine. It was also easy for me to act feminine when the situation required it, although I never preferred that behaviour.

I did not come out during a sudden, overwhelming moment of revelation, nor did I come out as a result of a natural, incremental process of awareness of lesbianism from childhood through adulthood. My first serious contact with lesbianism developed while I was participating in a government-sponsored, youth volunteer programme which spanned nine months in various parts of the country. The programme was called "Katimavik," and participants ranged in age from seventeen to twenty-one years. We were divided into groups of eleven or twelve participants from across the country and were guided by a leader. We lived communally in every sense: we worked on community-based projects together (environmental initiatives, daycare, work with seniors and the disabled, farm work, etc.); we lived together in one residence; we shared domestic duties as well as social/cultural activities. For three-month periods, in three different locations across the country, we lived together as "family."

There was a girl in my group who was three years my junior and whom I suspected was gay — or, at the very least, had strong tendencies. She was quite naïve in her behaviour toward other females. Had she realized how her behaviour was perceived by others — there were hushed comments and stated observations about her "weirdness" — I'm certain she would not have been so free. Part of her naïvete had to do with her comfortable, upper-middle-class, Prairie upbringing; and part of it was just due to her youth and inexperience — at eighteen, she was out on her own for the first time. In any case, whenever she was interacting, in her unself-conscious way, with the females in our group, the level of lesbian energy in the room would immediately rise. She would often become absorbed in quasi-philosophical conversations, and would cozily position herself in close proximity to her co-conversationalist, with eyes aglow. I had witnessed this oddity more than once and had often wondered how she could act in that way while other group members wandered about.

I didn't think I was a lesbian myself until after the programme was finished, so I was not self-aware enough during those nine months to even consider that I might be bisexual. Instead, I began seriously entertaining the thought of playing "cat and mouse" type games with my fellow participant. I felt that it would be a dare and be fun: a welcome change from my daily, predictable, service- and work-related activity, which was devoid of any hint of individuality or passion-driven desire. In the situation that developed over the next several months, I had the upper hand because I was the older one, from the big city, "exotic-looking," strong-minded and fiercely independent. I was also "street-smart," so I recognized early on that she was probably destined to become a lesbian, yet I never considered that I might share the same destiny. I just enjoyed "knowing" — or at least "suspecting" — her. I actively began scheming up situations that would draw her closer to me in a psycho-emotional sense, while I remained "safe" because I was controlling things. I was the more knowledgeable and, most important, I was able to impose limits at any moment.

Our involvement (it never turned into a full-blown relationship due to my "fear of the unknown" and foolish pride) began in an adversarial way, through an argument that erupted when we were bunking together during the initial orientation phase. The argument was over the proper way to wax a floor. She asserted herself with a haughty air, I asserted myself with genuine concern; she became rudely dismissive and more haughty, I exploded. From that time on, I made it a point to regard her as insignificant in my life and set out to solidify that decision by ignoring and avoiding her as much as possible.

In the beginning, it was hard because virtually all of our co-participants sided with my adversary's exaggerated version of events. She was insecure and accustomed to getting her own way. The more autonomous and self-reliant I became (immersing myself in my work, seeking stimulation outside my group, making it a point to be the better one at accomplishing tasks), the more other members of our group grew uneasy about my seeming lack of interest in the group and ability to function well without their support.

Eventually, every member of my group came around to accepting and liking me for who I was, despite their former prejudices — except, of course, her. She could not bring herself to admit that she might have been wrong. Besides, she must have felt like a fool after thinking she had succeeded in influencing the others for so long. It was at this point that I felt I had come out on top without unnecessarily ingratiating myself with anyone. It was definitely a significant feeling of power for me. It was empowering to know that, without intending to, I could gain the trust and friendship of the others. It was then that I decided to snub my adversary intentionally and play "mind-games" with her. I began to be able to hurt her feelings, and she began to give too much importance to my opinions. I played with her mind and enjoyed it. Sweet revenge!

To make a long story short, as the programme approached its end, I began to feel regret — mostly that I had never forgiven this woman and that I had not made friends with her. I had made her suffer, but I was too high on myself to stop. I let it go on for far too long. The closer the end of the programme came, the stronger my feelings of regret and my desire to make amends. Still, with just days to go before leaving, my pride prevented me from reaching out to her in genuine sincerity. It would have been too much, too late — an "emotionally loaded" gesture. I opted to play it safe on the day of departure, and managed only an ineffectual handshake followed by a quick "good-bye."

It was after arriving home that I realized I actually missed her and would continue to do so for longer than I cared to admit. I started to analyze the dynamics of the "relationship" and seriously owned up to the fact that I had been moved by this woman sexually — in particular, by her vulnerability in the face of my willfulness. On my initiative, we made several long-distance calls to each other and I accepted her invitation to come see her for a week during our mutual school breaks, but nothing ever happened. It was very strange. All the good intentions, longing and privacy were there — we were just too cautious with each other because of the past. Within weeks of returning from my visit, I actively set out to meet a "real lesbian" and to have the experience that I had subconsciously desired but only toyed with.

I did not know that Carol, my married sister with two young teens, was gay. I thought she was satisfied with her marriage. By the time I unexpectedly found out about Carol, I was fully involved in monthly visits to the local gay bar and determined to move on from my first real relationship (I had not been ready for it). I did not know that Carol knew I was gay (my younger sister, who was initially closer to Carol, had told her), so I was stunned and uncomfortable when we met face to face in the local bar.

I remember being dressed up and expectant and entering with a confident air, alert to any attractive inquiring looks. Before I even reached the bar to sit down, I heard someone call out confidently, and somehow familiarly, "Diana!" I remember being startled and stopping dead in mid-stride. I looked frantically around to find this person who obviously knew me so well, and discovered to my surprise and embarrassment that it was my sister Carol! My mind was churning with ways to deal with the immediate revelation. I finally decided to "play it cool" and demand to know what she was doing there in order to divert the interest away from me. She was with some friends and light-heartedly replied something to the effect of: "What do you think I'm doing here?"

I couldn't believe she was a lesbian — and I really didn't want to, because I was so convinced about her status as my married sister. I was not ready to believe that she could be gay — occasionally bisexual, perhaps, but not a convert. There had never been any evidence or reason to believe she could be lesbian; everything pointed toward heterosexuality. She was married with kids, for crying out loud! At any rate, I chatted with her for a while after she reassured me that it was true and that she was okay with my being a lesbian and keeping it secret from the rest of the family. I remember staying for a short while in her company because I was not quite yet over my feeling of embarrassment. Also, I was eager to make myself available to suitable women. I chatted with her while the place began to fill up, and then I went about my business.

Everyone in my family now knows that I am a lesbian. The first person to know was my youngest sister; she was and still is very supportive. She has even accompanied me to various gay events. Of course, my mother knows, and has for years. She found out by accident through a letter from my former first love. She begrudgingly accepts it now, but there has been no need to talk about it in detail. I won't allow it. My experience with my mother is that, if given too much information, she'll use it against me in the future to her advantage. My brothers know and they're fine with it — they believe in "live and let live." My younger brother is very open-minded. He has encouraged me to be more natural with him and has accompanied me to the bar in brotherly support.

Being out to my family, especially Carol, has provided me with more opportunities to get to know people within my circle in an open, non-threatening way. The fact that Carol and I are both gay has facilitated a better understanding of each other. We have something of significance in common, and that is what I appreciate most about our relationship.

Eva Borgström
and Gunnel Borgström

Translated by Maria Göransson

Eva

Gunnel

Sisterly
Reunion

We grew up in a middle-class family, in a mid-size town in the middle of Sweden. Borlänge was a typical industrial town; the biggest employers were the paper mill and the iron mill. When we were kids, there was no possibility for a higher education in Borlänge. If you wanted to study, you had to go to one of the university towns.

Many of our childhood friends chose to stay in Borlänge and to work, buy a house, start a family. Forming a family was probably a necessity for those who stayed in Borlänge. To live there alone or — even worse — as a lesbian, would have been almost unthinkable.

We had a house in a beautiful area on the outskirts of town. You could strap on your skis by the door and ski directly out into the forest. Our dad drew the plans for the house himself, and it is quite different from all the other homes in the area. Its shape was influenced by an argument with a neighbour. This neighbour, together with local authorities, was able to halt our first house plan, which was fairly conventional. He stated that the house would disturb his view of the church. Our dad, angry over the failure of the first plan, drew a new plan that the authorities passed. But he incorporated his irritation into the design, and the house became rather eccentric.

There are four children in our family — three girls and one boy. Mom worked at home throughout our entire childhood. Before she married, she had been a dancer at theatres in Stockholm and had sometimes worked as an extra in films. She ceased working as a dancer and extra when her first child was born, but the traditional chores for women never excited her and she felt isolated as a housewife in little Borlänge. When the children became older, she wanted to start a new career; but that never happened.

Dad is a civil engineer, but worked as a high-school teacher until he got his pension a few years ago. He never became too involved with his job — only to the extent that it was necessary. He immersed himself in his hobbies, though: hunting, fishing and sports. He always tried to convince the rest of the family to join him on nature walks and or the sports field. Mom and two of our siblings were pretty resistant to all the persuasion attempts — most of the time, they refused. He was more successful with his two lesbian daughters, though. We both enjoyed sports and we joined Dad on long fishing trips. Each year we had intense discussions about how to spend our vacation: abroad on a sunny beach, as Mom wanted; or in the mountains, as Dad wanted. We always went to the mountains.

Out of the four children in our family, the second and the fourth became lesbians. The first child was our big sister, Pia. If all the prejudices about lesbians were true, she should have been the lesbian daughter in the family. Often she is perceived as being manlike in her demeanour and dominant in her ways. But prejudices often do not coincide with reality: Pia is now married, has four children and is comfortable in her heterosexual identity.

Child number three, Ola, was the much-longed-for son. The plan was probably that he would be the one to participate in sports and become Dad's fishing partner, but he was just as uninterested in a sports career as Pia. He was more interested in wine, women and old cars. He seems to be the everlasting bachelor.

Both Pia and Ola now live up in a little village by the sea in the north of Sweden, where they enjoy life in the countryside and are each other's neighbours. It is ironic that these two, who never joined us on Dad's ten-hour nature excursions, chose to move to the country, where the forest and the sea are such important parts of life. It was the other two of us — the lesbian half of the children — who were fascinated by nature.

Among us children, it is pretty obvious that we stick together two and two: the first and the third child, and the second and the fourth child; or the two heterosexuals and the two lesbians; or however you want to describe it. All four of us maintain contact with one another, but everyday contact exists within the pairs. Pia and Ola moved 800 kilometres north, to a sparsely populated area, the older moving first and then the younger. We lesbians moved 500 kilometres south, to a big city — the older first and then the younger. If the two of us had not been lesbians, we probably would have ended up in the country, too; we are both deeply involved in environmental protection and we love nature. But it is still a bit difficult to imagine living as a lesbian in the countryside in Sweden, where so much revolves around the heterosexual family. Still, life is not over yet, and who knows where we will end up?

Left: Eva   Right: Gunnel

Eva

I have felt attracted to women for as long as I can remember. When I was a child, one crush on a girl was followed by another. Sometimes I felt a little something extra for a boy, too, but that was never as intense and it did not happen as often. I also may have constructed some of those stories about boys to please my girlfriends.

I was a tomboy who played soccer and "Cowboys and Indians" with the boys. There were only two other girls my age in our block, but they mostly played with each other. I think they had more in common with each other than with me — they both loved playing with dolls, and I did not.

When I was in second or third grade, it became obvious to me that I could not continue to behave in my customary manner. I realized that it was strange for a girl to dress as I did and be as boyish as I was. I stopped playing with the boys and, for a few years, I was pretty lonely.

When I was twelve, I found a new friend. Most of our contemporaries were practising their heterosexual womanhood. My friend and I felt that the roles for women — at least, those that we knew of — were totally impossible to live up to. Afterwards, we described those years as a time of "inner exile." Instead of becoming "real women," we sat around listening to music and had heated discussions. Together, we practised a different form of womanhood; we practised living as independent intellectuals. During high school, when we were fifteen or sixteen years old, we became involved in international solidarity projects. We hung out with a political youth group, and we finally felt that we had found other people who thought — and dressed — as we did. I also met a boy in the youth group and I had a three-year relationship with him. I had been observing this boy for a long time, and it came as a total surprise to me that he was interested in me, too. The problem was, at the very same time, I fell passionately in love with a woman. I think that this particular incident made me realize that I was definitely different: I had met a "dream prince," but fallen in love with a woman who did not even notice me.

After high school, I broke up with my boyfriend and moved away from home. During my first years in Göteborg, I was lost. I dated men, even though this was not satisfying. I didn't meet any lesbians or gay men; I felt alone. It was a few years before I finally came in contact with lesbians and I was twenty-four years old before I had a relationship with a woman for the first time.

My sister Gunnel was always special to me. She is so much younger than I that we never competed with each other. I remember being very happy when she was born. A friend of mine also got a little sister at the same time, and we used to play "Mother and Child" together; that was the only time during my childhood that I enjoyed that game. We took our little sisters for walks in strollers, fed them, changed their diapers and comforted them when they were sad.

My relationship with Gunnel was special also in another way. She was born during a time when I thought a lot about whether I was different or not. I never saw other girls dress or act the way I did. Gunnel was the first child who provided a mirror for me. She was a happy little savage — her hair was a mess, her clothes were often dirty and her knees were always scraped. She was just the way I remembered I had been!

When I moved to Göteborg, I did not have much contact with my family for a few years. But I remember how happy Gunnel was when I came home and how we used to play together. She always stuck close to me and, at night, she wanted me to read to her or play the guitar — even though, whenever I did that, she became so alert that she could not sleep.

When she became an adult, met her boyfriend and moved away from home, we grew apart. We had more contact with each other when she moved to Göteborg, but we still did not see each other very often. She was playing sports and socializing in her heterosexual student groups. I did research and mostly socialized with other lesbians. We seldom met each others' friends. We lived different lives.

Once, she came with me to a women's party. I remember wondering what she would think when she saw that many of the women were lesbians and danced with each other. To my surprise, she enjoyed herself very much. She was only supposed to come for a short time because she had to get up early the next morning, but she stayed a lot longer than she had planned. The same thing happened a few years later, at my celebration when I received my doctorate — but she will tell that story herself. I was surprised both times. She had lived up to the trappings of heterosexual femininity so much better then I had ever done, and I had forgotten the feeling of recognition that I had experienced when I had observed Gunnel as a child.

Front: Gunnel   Back: Eva

Gunnel

When I read Eva's description of her childhood, I immediately identify with two things. I, too, played "Cowboys and Indians" and soccer with the boys instead of playing with the girls who liked dolls. I remember that, when I was in fourth or fifth grade, I was shut out by the boys in my class because I was so tough and dominant. I was very upset about that and adapted myself by withdrawing and becoming more careful. This is still true. I seldom fight with people; I am pretty scared of conflicts and I rarely become angry.

I am the youngest child in my family — the runt of the litter — and was probably not planned. I do not remember much about my elder sisters from my childhood since they all moved out when I was around seven. Most of my growing-up years were spent with my brother. Later, when he moved out too, I was alone with my parents. I do have a few strong childhood memories of all of us as a family, though.

One memory is of ordinary days when the whole family was home after school and work, and we were all in the kitchen. If the radio played a happy and swingy tune, a wild dance — some strange sort of jitterbug — would break out, involving all the children. I, the smallest, flew between my sisters' and brother's arms and legs. It was wonderful!

I also remember that the one who always talked to me and comforted me when I was sad was my sister Eva. I remember having close contact with her, and that memory is validated when I see old pictures, in many of which I sit close to her. After she and my other sister, Pia, moved to Göteborg at the same time, many years passed before we had close contact again. During those years we saw each other only at Christmas and on summer vacations. And, during those years, a lot happened to both of us.

I was probably the child who was most able to live up to our father's expectations. I got a degree in science and played sports on a national level. From the age of thirteen or fourteen until the time I was twenty-six, my life revolved around school, practices, homework, travelling, competitions, food and sleep. I lived a very hectic life, with not much time for emotions.

When I was seventeen, I realized for the first time that I was in love with a woman — my new classmate and very good friend. Of course, I was shaken by this experience, but I never thought about it as a problem. I never talked to anyone about it; I merely accepted the fact that I was comfortable with men in general and with my boyfriend, whom I had recently met, in particular.

I cannot remember if, at that specific time, I knew that Eva was a lesbian. But it certainly was around then that my brother, Ola, told me the news. My reaction to Eva's "bent" was simply a calm acceptance of the fact; it did not upset me at all. To me, she was still the warm sister she always had been. It did not matter if she chose to live with men or with women.

Ten years passed. I moved away from home when I was eighteen and lived with my boyfriend; we stayed together for eight more years. During that time, I studied for three years at the university in Göteborg, then went on to Kalmar to do my last year and got my degree as a biologist. I had luck and immediately got a job with a research project in Kalmar. At the same time, I travelled around Sweden and around the world, playing table tennis. I was able to maintain the relationship with my boyfriend, to whom I was now engaged. And I occasionally fell in love with women, but never did anything about it.

Then, when I was twenty-five or twenty-six, I had a crisis. The whole thing started with a serious knee injury that forced me to give

Gunnel

up my sports career. I spent a lot of time at the hospital and I thought about my life — where I was going and why I was feeling so unhappy.

During this time of reflection, something happened that would have a great impact on my life: Eva received her doctorate. Even before this, I had thought her life and friends were exciting. At the party to celebrate her doctorate, about thirty lesbians showed up. The party was a great success, with lots of creative and beautiful lesbians, who sang and played music. I was enchanted! After a sleepless night of inner chaos, I decided to break up with my boyfriend and move back to Göteborg. I knew I had to explore this enticing life.

Six months passed before I was able to complete the break-up with my boyfriend. Looking back, I think this was the most difficult part of my coming-out process. He was the finest man I had ever met and I was very sad that he could not make me happy. When I told Eva about the break-up, she asked me why I had reached my decision. I vaguely tried to explain, and that was the first time I tried to put words to my feeling that I might be a lesbian.

In the fall of 1992, I was back in Göteborg. I had left everything — my job, my sports career, my boyfriend and all my heterosexual friends in Kalmar were now behind me. A few emotionally stormy years followed. For the first time, I experienced being passionately in love, with all that this includes. I opened my heart wide and experienced heavenly heights and deep valleys. I still become very confused when my common sense cannot curb my emotions and I behave like an idiot. But I do not mind that confusion. I am happy; I feel alive and I am not a robot exercising full control over my emotions any more. If it had not been for my sister Eva and her exciting world, I doubt that I ever would have found the way.

Joy McBride
and Karen McBride

Left: Joy   Right: Karen

Answering to My Sister's Name

Karen

I am the eldest of four kids, which is, in itself, a unique position in a family, creating ties and responsibilities that play out throughout childhood and beyond. But I'm only the eldest by eight minutes. That's eight loooong, and important minutes when you are a kid in grade school trying to assert yourself as unique and existing apart from your twin sister. As much as I tried to stretch them out, the eight minutes weren't always enough of a time span to warrant a unique identity — or, at least, it felt like that. But, just like binoculars, you could flip those precious eight minutes around and there was ample distance to make me feel like I was the older one, who had the responsibility of looking after my younger twin sister.

Although Joy and I were never purposefully dressed alike in our pre-teen years, it was difficult to avoid the similarities and the sharing. When snowsuits went on sale, we got to choose between the brown one and the blue one, with the same fur-lined hoods. We had identical sleeping bags, sneakers, bikes, baseball gloves, and the "same but different" Sunday outfits (my blue pants and red top contrasted with Joy's red pants and blue top). I don't think the similarities were without good

— even practical — reason, in most cases. What parents in their right mind would troop through the stores twice, with two kids in tow, when they had finally found what they needed? And why pass up gifts that came in sets of matching twos when they were badly needed? No matter how hard our parents tried to make us different, by varying colours and giving us choices, we sometimes couldn't help but be carbon copies or mirror images of each other.

On the positive side, I never did any of the terrible firsts on my own. My first day of school was shared with Joy, along with the first trips to camp and to the dentist, and our first music recital. To this day, I still slip up and say "we" when I'm trying to refer to just myself. The whole is not only greater than the sum of the parts, but more ingrained and more pervasive.

Despite the similar snowsuits, identical oxfords and same first trip to camp, Joy did graduate work in history and I graduated with a B.Sc. in engineering. I couldn't spell (Joy did the editing for this piece) and she had to call me to calculate the area of a triangle. I played field hockey and she excelled at basketball. She could read a book in the time it took me to lap the block on my roller skates, and I rebuilt my first car engine at age seventeen. The list of our differences is as long as the litany of commonalities. Despite the differences, the bond with my twin sister is tighter than any other family bond, and the feeling of sameness that it creates is very real for me.

When I was in my early twenties, I came to the realization that I was a lesbian. At the time, this was uniquely mine. I cherished the fact that it was something apart from Joy, something that I didn't have to share. In fact, I wasn't suppose to tell anyone. It was perfect! Now I had an identity, a group of friends, places to go and a secret in which Joy had no part. There was no bond. It was mine, it was me. I caught myself skipping down the street whistling Sesame Street's "One of these things is not like the other. One of these things just doesn't belong." What luck! I thought. Being a lesbian established instant boundaries, which I didn't have to work to define. Society said that no one would choose to be party to something as undesirable as homosexuality. When I worked up the courage to tell Joy I was a lesbian, I knew that my new identity would not be compromised by my having to share it like I had had to share my first day at school.

It was four years and eight minutes later when Joy told me that she, too, was a lesbian. I was underwhelmed, then disappointed. Finally I had made my getaway, only to find that I had escaped back into the same yard, with the two identical bikes, the ball gloves and matching oxfords. My boundaries and uniqueness instantly dissolved. Being the lone lesbian in the family had defined me, and the secretive nature of being gay had shown me where I could take the chalk and draw the line. Now, with one sentence, Joy was erasing those lines.

I had no desire to be included in the conversation when Joy told my parents that she was a lesbian. I had done it for myself and that was hard enough. I wasn't about to be there when the last daughter proclaimed her lesbianism and put to rest the hopes for a big wedding and the accompanying hunt for matching china. Out of fear, and in the name of avoidance, I started the second and more complete severing of the whole into the sum of the parts. I told Joy that she was going to have to tell Mom and Dad on her own. I didn't go. My fore and aft support was minimal. She did it on her own and I heard about it second-hand.

Since then, Joy and I have both worked to establish who we are, independent of the other. Life has dished up polar realities for us, and we have faced them, incorporated them into our relationship and identities, and carried on from there. Joy is on a disability pension now and I work as a computer programmer. We live about 400 kilometres apart, she in her rented apartment and me in my old house. We phone each other regularly and see each other four or five times a year. We now share our lesbianism like we once did the similar snowsuits. Both are identical outer shells that hold two very different people inside. Now the eight minutes are a reminder that we shared the cramped, warm space in the womb — and that some part of us is always touching.

Joy

Earlier this year, I watched news reports about twin girls in Toronto who had been born joined at the head and were being operated upon. I know they were too young to be speaking and sharing feelings — acts that we, as adults, count as signs of closeness. But I have a picture in my head of them reaching up to touch each other after the surgery, and finding only empty space. I imagine them meeting their discovery with such a profound sense of loss and bewilderment: the person they'd experienced as an extension of themselves was really a separate being — someone who could be taken away. The weaker of the two was taken away — she died sometime later.

It made me wonder about my relationship with my sister, about what being a twin really means. I feel very separate and distinct from Karen now — occasionally even distanced and removed. After all, I have always felt our differences have marked us out much more than our commonalities. Yet I think back to those twins on television, and although I know we weren't joined biologically, as they were, I figure there must be something from the physical closeness of our early years together, and the constant company we kept, that links us up.

I know that, as kids, both of us always cried when one of us was hurt or upset. I remember one summer day, when I'd been cut on the chin. I walked into the kitchen crying for Mom, and Karen followed me with such a noisy stream of tears that Dad grabbed her and turned her around, looking to see where the blood was. He was sure she had been cut, too. I find that I confuse her with me when I try to remember past events, so that I'm left wondering what really happened to whom. Was it me who was in that hospital bed or Karen? Was the girl in the next bed — the one with the hole in her back — someone I'm remembering through my eyes or through Karen's? And how come I can see Dad yelling at her upstairs in our bedroom, when I know I was outside, standing in the driveway at the time? Can I really have absorbed what Karen felt to the point where her experiences became my memories? Would these kind of links be there if we hadn't been the same age?

We weren't identical twins, and were very different emotionally and physically as children. I was tall and skinny; Karen was shorter and stronger. We both grew up playing sports, but Karen had the quick reflexes of a goalie, whereas I had the fluidity and speed of a runner. I did well in school and loved to read and write. Karen didn't; she liked the precision of sciences and maths and was much happier working on bikes and cars than she was doing anything sedentary. She was much more social than I was and got into the high-school scene of dating boys and partying in a way that I never did. I was something of a loner. I tended to have only one close friend at a time, and when I did go out with Karen and her friends it was more likely than not because Mom had told her to bring me along.

Left: Joy   Right: Karen

I was pretty unhappy at this time. In elementary school I remember having a sense that there was something very wrong with me. I interpreted this deep unhappiness and sense of culpability as a type of birth defect. I believed that I had been born without whatever it was that made someone a lovable person — that this was, indeed, a characteristic one either got or didn't and I had missed out. I remember knowing this to the point where I took for granted any ill treatment I received as something I justly deserved rather than as a situation that could have been changed if I had known how to speak up for myself. Karen was much more argumentative than I was. I remember her getting into some awful fights, both in the school yard and with my parents. She knew how to defend herself. I just tried to never make waves, to never get anyone angry.

As adults, these differences in temperament and interest took us in very separate directions. We went to different universities, I to study history and Karen to study engineering. After school, she spent a number of years working as a mechanic, then switched to computer work. During this period, she was involved in long-term relationships with women, though I very naïvely thought she and her "roommates" just didn't have enough space or money for two beds. (Honestly.) I didn't know what she felt about herself or about me then. I don't remember us talking very openly with each other about our feelings as kids, and I think we grew even more emotionally distant as adults, even though we stayed in constant contact.

I spent some time working as a cook after my first degree, and then went back to school to do graduate work. I became even more isolated as an adult. By then, I'd perfected strategies for hiding how unhappy I was. I used a talent for being funny to entertain acquaintances, hid behind Karen when I could, and took great pains to avoid socializing, even if it meant lying or being rude to people. I spent most of my free time either alone or with family members. Since I had stayed in more than Karen had as a teenager, I was the one who had been asked to look after my brothers when my parents were out. This role continued even after I'd left home, as I hadn't travelled as far away to university as Karen had. I got used to being the one called upon during emergencies and, as these were very crisis-filled years for our family, I spent a lot of time looking after relatives or mediating their disputes, and very little time trying to figure out how to solve my own problems.

It was my coming out that began to change all of this. I came out to myself the day I found out that Karen was a lesbian. I remember reading the letter she had sent me and then sitting down on the kitchen floor and starting to cry. I wasn't upset that she was a lesbian; I was upset because I knew in my gut that that explained what I was too, and I had no idea what to do with that information.

There had never been any talk about homosexuality around our house. We had a close relative who was a lesbian, but no one ever talked about her sexual orientation and she remained closeted until she died not too long ago. Before my sister came out to me, I had never met anyone who was out. This isn't surprising, considering how hard I had worked to isolate myself socially. I had grown up with the theory that I was unlovable, and this stuck with me as an adult so strongly that it never occurred to me to think that I might instead be a lesbian — one who had been brought up in a world that hadn't taught me how to recognize or cherish myself.

I spent years slowly building friendships with some lesbians and a gay man I happened to meet through school before I finally came out to them. I remember fearing, even then, that they might spot me as a pretender, as someone who was really just unlovable and who wanted to pass herself off as something better than what she was. I got so much support from them that my self-esteem just soared. My social life definitely improved and I eventually ended up in a long-term relationship. It was one of the happiest periods of my life, and being a lesbian is still one of the rock-solid good things I know about myself.

Karen and I were still pretty distant with each other at this point. I have no memory of coming out to her — something I think is telling, since I remember all my other coming-outs very clearly. She would have been the first family member I told. I know that, in general, she was upset with me and I remember that her partner did a lot of mediating between the two of us. Finally, Karen's partner got fed up playing go-between and forced Karen and me to talk directly to each other. That was the day we started building a new relationship. So, in my eyes, if being twins kept us in constant contact throughout our lives, despite our emotional distance, then being lesbians is what got us talking.

It hasn't always been easy. Karen and I struggled through a lot as we measured out a new relationship and worked out problems we'd had with each other and with family. I feel as if it's a constant, this balancing out of fear and distrust, with love, laughter and the draw of old ties. This twin sister of mine, who is not very much like me, can even seem like a stranger to me at times. Yet I also feel that she somehow lives inside my skin, so that even though I know we're separate people, I can still end up feeling taken aback by our differences and by the times when we lack the ability to understand each other.

The changes are definitely there, though. I've seen them over the past few years: when Karen called to talk to me about a relationship that had ended; when I called to talk to her when mine ended too; when I started talking to her about abuse I remembered experiencing as a child, something I had always kept a secret from her before.

But there's one thing that hasn't changed, something that marks me out as a twin, that tells me part of her will stick with me forever. I noticed it when the editor of this book called me "Karen" during a phone call and I didn't bother to correct her. I still answer to my sister's name.

Gail Hewison, Jane Waddy and Libby Silva

Left: Gail   Centre: Libby   Right: Jane

We Three — Her, She and Me

Gail

Introducing three lesbian sisters from Sydney, Australia: me, Gail (fifty-four); Jane (forty-seven); and Libby (forty-two). All three of us came out in the mid-'70s, during the height of the Women's Liberation Movement. Before we got together thirteen years ago to run a bookshop, we had each been involved in a variety of feminist endeavours: health centres, abortion counselling, child-abuse work. Before becoming a feminist, I had worked in advertising/fashion, while Jane was a teacher and Libby worked in travel. For the last thirteen years we have run The Feminist Bookshop in Sydney. We were able to buy the bookshop from the original owners in 1982, when our aunt died and left us a small inheritance. We put all of it into the bookshop, had a few difficult years of learning a completely new line of work and now have a very successful business that we all love.

When we were all children, I adored my little sisters — they were both so cute and pretty. Jane had long blonde hair, and I remember doing her braids when she started school. We all went to the same girls-only school and were close as children, in spite of a big age difference. As the oldest sister, I often had to take care of my siblings, which made me feel important. I think I grew up too fast, however, and felt overly responsible. I also had to face heavy expectations from inexperienced parents. I was the first to do everything and had to negotiate with my parents over things that probably came easier for my younger sisters. I remember Jane and Libby thanking me for wearing my parents down. At eighteen, when Libby was just out of kindergarten, I left school and went to teachers' college; then, at twenty, I married and left home. I missed being involved in my sisters' teenage years.

I'm sure our relationships with one another have been affected by our order of birth. In adult life I have certainly tried to move out of the older-sister role. This was especially important to do if we were to work as three equal partners in our business. Difficulties usually arise over control, when one or the other of us steps over a boundary or thinks someone else has! Being a "Bossy Boots" is a family trait. Issues generally get worked out, though, and, no matter what the difficulty is, we have great trust in one another and work together very well. And, although we spend a lot of time together at work, we also have very different interests and social groups. Running the bookshop together has meant we've had to resolve issues. Luckily, we share certain ways of thinking and communicating that make us very intuitive and sensitive to one another. We will often arrive at work and find that we have all dressed in the same colour. I enjoy our shared sense of humour; we can communicate it at a glance.

In the bookshop, we each have particular areas of expertise and respect the others' skills. Libby has the neatest writing I have ever seen and keeps the books immaculately, and as well as any account-ant. Jane has boundless energy for work — she no sooner thinks of an idea before it is done. My talents lie in public relations and networking with other organizations through such things as news-letters. We co-operate over holidays — when one of us is away, the other two pull together and willingly do more work. In this way, it's been possible for all of us to have substantial holiday breaks and overseas trips during the years we've worked together. We also employ five other women, who share the workload with us.

Having two lesbian sisters has been great for me. Coming out was not quite so difficult as it could have been. I came out in 1976, at age thirty-six. My change of consciousness was like a big spiritual awakening: feminism and lesbianism together, in one exciting pack-age. I had previously been married, widowed, married again and divorced, and in all those years it had never crossed my mind that I was a lesbian. When I came out and looked back, I could see how my lesbianism had always been there. I had not been able to recognize it because of my society's and family's expectations of me in the very repressed '50s and '60s. Lesbianism was all but invisible then, and definitely not an acceptable choice.

Soon after I came out, my youngest sister, Libby, told me she had known from the age of eleven that she was a lesbian and had consciously suppressed this information. Being twelve years younger than me, she had found it slightly easier not to succumb to society's pressures and had not married, even though she had long-term relationships with men. She came out at the age of twenty-four. Our middle sister, Jane, came out few years later, after several long "het" relationships. Feminism had a huge impact on us all and is still central to our lives.

I sometimes feel amazed at my good fortune in having lesbian sisters. Upon occasion, our mother has blamed me for starting it all and influencing the others, but, as we are very positive about our lives, she seems to accept our lesbianism and often says she is very proud of us. We have quite a few cousins, but I don't know of any other gays or lesbians in the family. There were a lot of unmarried aunts and uncles in my grandparents' generation, and the old family photos hint at many mysteries. One of our grandmothers was a suffragist and instilled a lot of early feminist ideas into members of the family. We also have a brother who is a busy fashion photographer with an ex-wife, a girlfriend and a daughter. They are all very supportive of me, and my brother has always had lots of gay friends. When I was arrested in 1978 at the first Gay and Lesbian Mardi Gras in Sydney, he came into the city at midnight to bail me out and joined the night-long demonstration with my sisters and gay and lesbian friends. My partner/lover Liz is an only child and envies my relationships with my two lesbian sisters and large family.

If I had been the only lesbian in the family, I think I could have had a very difficult time and probably would have isolated myself. However, with my two sisters coming out soon after I did, my parents tried very hard to be accepting as they didn't want to lose all three daughters. Mum and Dad have always had the attitude that, if their children are happy, then they are happy. During the recent break-up of my sister Libby's long-term relationship, my mother was very supportive and is herself grieving over the loss of her daughter-in-law. My dad is now suffering from Alzheimer's but has always been very fond of all the "girls" — although he used to grumble sometimes at being surrounded by so many women.

Many of our lesbian friends are completely incompatible with their siblings and think it's pretty amazing that the three of us are all lesbians and feminists, working together and liking one another. I certainly count this situation as one of the blessings of my life — to have two lesbian sisters who are also my friends.

Jane

Is three a crowd or isn't it? It has been in our family …
we've mostly been two to one, but the two keeps
changing. It wasn't that we excluded each other —
that's just the way it flowed.

I remember the day Libby was born. I hung out of
the car window, eating almonds, waiting for Mum and
the baby to wave to me from the fourth floor of the
hospital. Lib and I were inseparable and played cubby
houses from then on. We must have been very small,
because we could slither between the legs of the
kitchen stool.

We had two grandmothers, both of whose partners
had died. Grandma was very strong and intellectual.
Nan was strong and tramped the paddocks in old
muddy boots, scattering the chooks. Our aunts were
all fascinating and funny, and our uncles adored them.
Mum was always the one who said "yes" or "no." Dad
would leave washing the dishes to waltz her around the
room.

Gail let me sleep in her room once when Santa was
coming. She ate the sandwiches I put out for him and
said, "Don't worry about it." She gave me a cigar box to
put my pencils in. She was full of mystery.

Back: Gail   Left: Libby   Right: Jane

My brother taught me to play marbles and to box. We had bleeding noses for years. He and I crept around, eating big slabs of butter, and he protected me from being kicked by his friend, Richard, who grew into a gynaecologist.

Gail, Lib and I went to a school for young ladies. There were 600 girls and about fifty woman teachers. I had a crush on a few of each. One girl was more than a crush. I liked all the teachers, especially the ones we identified as lesbians. The best teacher had masses of hair under her arms. We tortured her for it. I remember the look on Sexy Lexie's face when she hauled six of us out of a cupboard where we had set up a club to discuss periods, boys and our legs, instead of going to class. Gail was very interested in this, as she had also had a cupboard experience. The teachers probably wondered if they had a genetic problem on their hands — they certainly watched Libby closely.

While Dad taught me to waterski, Lib and her girlfriend locked themselves away, busily dressing and undressing Barbie — and undressing her again. Meanwhile, Gail was having fun with her girlfriends; they were pushing and laughing so much that one of them crashed through a glass door. Ten minutes after her arm was stitched up, they all threw themselves, hilarious with glee, into the sea. What were they up to? Lib and I wanted to know.

Gail spent one summer teaching me French — all about Madame Souris *et ses filles*. Meanwhile, Lib and I raced backwards and forwards to the library, devouring the Bobbsey Twins. We also spent afternoons in coffee shops eating cake with Mum — something strictly forbidden by the school. It was great! The smell of dry-cleaning fluid on woollen tunics was not! I taught Lib to surf; she was so sweet, bouncing over the waves. Then her ovarian cyst burst ... we both had one out, as a matter of fact.

Gail would never lend me her hairbrush, however desperate I was. But she did take me to the snow and taught me to ski. My boyfriend and I took her to see the musical *Hair*. She took my boyfriend! We swapped a couple of men, actually.

In the '70s, I worked in a psychiatric hospital. Most of my friends were lesbian or gay. It didn't occur to me that I might be, too, or that they should be different. They were all confident, clever and out.

Lib and I went to Bali and Fiji. Gail and I drove up the east coast of Australia. We ran our car under a truck up to its windscreen, our laps and mouths full of salami, cheese and bread rolls: To be killed while stuffing our faces would have been humiliating.

We did a lot of eating together, Gail, Lib and I. We left our boyfriends at home and went to Paris together, where we ate so many croissants and babas that we had a cranky attack. Lib and I packed Gail onto the train to London to stay with two lesbian friends. Then, Lib and I went holidaying with two other lesbian friends. Lesbians were everywhere. But we weren't lesbians! After I got over my sugar attack, I felt bad for the next twenty-five years for pushing Gail onto the train alone. She told me only this week that all she had felt was incredible relief to get away from us!

I don't think I remember when Gail became a lesbian. She just seemed to spend more time with women. I was there when Lib told Mum and Dad that she was a lesbian. Mum gave her such an opening line. It was Lib's thirtieth birthday and Mum said: "Oh, Libby, this time thirty years ago you were just about to come out!" There wasn't much of a fuss, really. I always felt that there was more fuss and bother about my boyfriends, who never seemed to be quite suitable.

International Women's Year came with great excitement. In Sydney, the lesbians demanded to lead the parade. Gail and Lib had lots of friends I didn't know — one of them was wearing tampons for earrings. Some of my friends were affronted, but I thought it was fabulous.

At an early gay and lesbian march through Sydney, Gail was one of about fifty people arrested. I waited all night to bail her out, but she was really cross with me because I had asked our brother for help with money. She yelled at me in front of her friends. I was humiliated, but that was separatism. That's how it was back then.

When I was in the city with a friend a year later, another gay and lesbian march went past. I saw my two sisters and dragged my friend into the march. I said to her, "Well, we might be lesbians ourselves one day." She promptly got married and had two kids, but I know.

So I joined the Freeda Stares lesbian feminist tap-dancing group and started getting some exercise. I loved the cheering crowds, and I rather liked the girl with the beautiful eyes in the lesbian choir. Lib and I lived next door to each other, and one night I took some soup to her house. She was having a party and I was rather startled to find her home full of forty Radclyffe Halls. I didn't understand what they were up to, but I thought they all looked fantastic — Gail and Lib, in particular.

I went overseas with Lib and, when I came back, my boyfriend had found someone else. He said she was prettier, funnier, cleverer, and she washed her pubic hair with shampoo and conditioner ... what can you say to that! Gail looked after me. We took up drawing classes and I tap-danced my legs off.

Feminism was booming, and the lesbians were having the best fun. I had noticed that. Gail, Lib and I bought The Feminist Bookshop. The choirist with the beautiful eyes moved into the apartment upstairs. We got talking at the Hiroshima Day March and we've been together for eleven years! The first time we kissed, she threw her keys into the air in excitement. They were never seen again. She was locked out of her house, her car and her work. The four of us spent hours looking for those keys, but they never reappeared!

I think my parents were shocked about me being a lesbian: Now three out of three daughters were lesbian. I had been their last chance for another grandchild. What on earth was I doing? They made life very hard for me and my girlfriend, Jan. Lib and her girlfriend and Jan and I went to the beach and had picnics all the time, and Gail and her girlfriend were really lovely to us. They all thought it was terrific. My brother was fine about it. He was always a great support.

But something went wrong, and the closer Jan and I became, the less supportive Lib became, and I felt rejected. A long period of great pain overwhelmed me.

Writing this story has been very hard. It has brought back many quirky memories — the reasons why I love my sisters. But it has also led to considerable conflict among us, to do with control, anger, change and loss — the reasons why I sometimes feel furious with them. For me, these issues aren't resolved. Working together has meant that we have had to keep trying.

None of us can squeeze between the legs of the kitchen stool these days — but we are sisters and it's not all over yet.

Libby

When I was born, many years ago, my two sisters said, "Ooo, goodie, she's a lesbian!" Thus my life began. Well … it wasn't exactly like that, but all's well that ends well.

Gail was twelve and a half and Jane was nearly five when I was born. For some reason, Mum and Dad were hoping for another boy, whom they would call "Mark"; instead, they got me. And thank the Goddess they got me!

Our mother always congratulated herself about the choice she and my father made about him leaving the air force and studying medicine. She told us that they had made this choice so that their children would have a stable life and not grow up to be … probably what we indeed did grow up to be. Jane and I were inseparable from an early age, and Gail was the older, grown-up, wiser sister. I looked to Jane for fun and games, and we played together endlessly. I loved her. I don't know why, at the age of three, I took to her dresses with a pair of scissors. I guess I knew about hand-me-downs and already I was butch: no dresses for me, thank you very much. I was a very determined child and knew what I liked in the clothing department. Once, Gail came home from a holiday in sunny Queensland with a pair of "pedal-pushers" for me; they had a midriff top that showed my ribs. I was horrified to think that my sister did not know how much I would hate this outfit. My mother made me wear it, and it must have looked strange because I wore it with a singlet tucked into the pants. No one was going to see my belly.

My sisters were a great influence on my life. When we were seven and two, Jane and I were sent off to Adelaide for holidays with our grandmother, aunt and uncle. I would look to Jane for guidance and would eat only what she approved of — Vegemite sandwiches and tinned peaches. Jane also taught me to squeeze the first inch of toothpaste down the drain because "dirty little boys have sucked it." This was possibly the beginnings of feminism for me. In contrast, Gail came home from New York and had us sitting on the edge of the bath, arms outstretched, applying depilatory cream to our unsightly hairs. And it was Gail who urged us both to shave our legs. We all laugh about it now, as we accept our natural hairy state!

I knew from a young age that I loved girls and women. At about the age of ten I went to see the movie *Lawrence of Arabia* and, at dinner that night, I told my family how I hated it because there was not one woman in the entire film. I remember Gail scoffing at me for even noticing this fact, and I realized then that I would have to be very, very careful not to let the cat out of the bag.

Menstruation came as a big shock to me. I found it very hard to understand how this dreadful thing that was happening to me had also happened to my sisters — and they hadn't warned me about it. After about six months of getting my period, I was shocked yet again to realize that my sisters were still getting their periods and that it didn't end by the time you became nineteen. How could this be true? I felt sick.

I remember the first time we communicated deeply and honestly. The three of us were lying on a beach, and Gail told us that, some time before, she had had an abortion. I was shocked that this had happened in the past and that there was nothing I could do about it — no chance of her changing her mind, no chance to support her decision, and no niece. I felt sad not to be an aunt. None of us had children. I think this conversation was the beginning of our close relationship as adults.

When I grew up, I became proud of my sisters and our shared life. It hasn't always been easy and untroubled, but we have an ongoing relationship of great depth and love. Gail was the first to come out as a lesbian and, initially, I felt troubled by her lesbianism. But I had great admiration for, and attraction to, her lover and this helped me to accept my sister's sexuality. It gave me the courage to look at my own life. It wasn't long before I had a lesbian affair and I've never looked back.

On my thirtieth birthday I decided to come out to my parents. I invited Jane to the occasion, too. It was to happen in one of Sydney's landmarks — the revolving restaurant in Centerpoint Tower — over lunch. I had warned Jane that I would be "coming out." By the time lunch was over, I still hadn't spoken the necessary words and my father was preparing to go. I said we should have coffee, as we'd probably never come there again. Jane and I looked deeply into each other's eyes and I took courage in her presence; I told my parents about being a lesbian. It was one of the most moving experiences of my life. My mother and I cried, and Dad leapt up and said this was no place to be making a scene. He said it didn't matter what I was as long as I could spell! Jane told him to sit down and shut up and listen. I gave them a book on the subject and said how important it was for us to keep talking about it. Which we did.

I don't think it was long after that before Jane, too, fell in love — with the lesbian next door. It was a very exciting time for us three sisters; our lives became lavender, green and white. Both of my sisters have worked for the love of women. We all have. The first words on child sexual assault that I ever read were written by my sister Gail. She was one of the first Australian women to publish writings on child abuse, back in the '70s. We are all proud to be Lesbian Feminists; it is who we are and it is in our blood.

I have had times with both my sisters — at different times, fortunately — when I needed to go through a process of separation and to redefine my boundaries. These have been occasions of excruciating pain and angst. I have gone through therapy and counselling with both of them. It took courage and trust for all of us to go through this process. Today we live separate lives and have deep respect and love for one another. And they are my friends.

Karin Hergl
and Christiane Hergl

Translated by Susan Pratt

Left: Christiane   Right: Karin

Learning How to Be Sisters

Karin

I was born in Berlin in 1955. My mother lived in a two-and-a-half-room flat with her parents, while my father lived in Frankfurt, where he could work and earn money. Occasionally, he would came to Berlin to visit us. My grandparents' home was very cramped: In addition to my mother and me, my grandmother, my great-aunt Dina and my aunt Inge also lived there. In 1956, my sister, Christiane, was born. I have barely any conscious memory of this time, except that it was dismal.

In 1957, my parents got their own flat — two-and-a-half rooms in a new estate on the edge of the city. My father had found work in Berlin, and the family could finally live together. Family life brought with it role distribution: My mother stayed at home, was a house-wife and brought up her two daughters; my father went to work and didn't come home until evening. At first, my parents had an active social life with friends and acquaintances of my father's. There were lively Skat evenings, which were followed, the next morning, by ashtrays full to the brim and empty bottles. Everything would happen a little slower than usual that next day. Later, there were hardly any of these social events outside the family.

My mother's large family became our main social focal point. On weekends, we always visited each other or did something together. The central figure was my grandmother. She had her fingers in every pie and interfered in everything; this frequently caused bitter arguments.

I took after my father, and Christiane took after my mother. The official line was that our parents loved their daughters equally. In reality, things were different: I knew my father loved me but I often doubted if my mother really did.

I was a quiet child. Throughout my youth and into adulthood, people always said: "Karin is shy, she does not trust herself to say anything." How this came about, and whether or not it was so from the beginning, I really don't know. It was fear that made me silent, but the fear was never acknowledged and the subject was never broached. My family acted as if being so silent was my manner or my own decision. As a child, I could put up no resistance to them except with my silence and occasional violent outbreaks of anger.

My sister, Christiane, was responsible for speaking. She was a lively talker and was supported in this. My family liked to use opposites to describe us: Karin, the silent one, and Christiane, the cheeky one; Karin, the one with the straight dark hair, and Christiane, the one with the blonde curls; Karin, the bulky, unpleasant, resentful daughter, and Christiane, the friendly, nice, good-natured daughter. These were fixed descriptions — prejudices — and, in certain ways, they were also cages.

Our family constellation was not exactly designed to create a hearty, intimate sisterly relationship, whatever that may be. The family split us up; I was on my own. As the older, sensible sister, I was supposed to look after Christiane, to make sure she did not get up to any mischief. I resisted these duties. I felt that I had not only been given the unattractive tasks and assignments, I was also supposed to help my sister be seen in an even better light. I often refused to do this.

As soon as I went to school, I made my own friends, and these contacts to the world outside my family were crucial for me. I guarded them jealously and did not speak much about them at home. For me, family meant being forced into an unbearable corset, being harnessed and, finally, being extinguished.

I always had at least one best friend with whom I could speak about the important matters of life. I made a great effort to avoid any mixing between my friends and my family, and I avoided any open struggles in relationships. I did not want to lose. In 1975, when I began university, I moved out of home and, for a long time, had no close contact with Christiane. We each knew what the other was doing, but that was all; we each went our own way.

I first got back in contact with Christiane in 1981, as I was just about to have my first lesbian experience after a long relationship with a man. Christiane spoke to me about being a lesbian and told me about her lesbian tendencies, which I had previously known nothing about. That was a great surprise and a great joy. I had not thought that anything would ever bind us except the family. I had believed that Christiane and my family were closed chapters in my life.

When our parents found out that we were lesbians, they each reacted differently. My mother reproached herself for bringing us up incorrectly, while my father veiled himself in silence. I was not present when our parents told others that we were lesbians; it was not spoken about openly. I was forced to confront, once again, the lack of communication in our family. I wished they had reacted with happiness, support or recognition of our courage in placing ourselves outside the normal world. Christiane often confronted our parents with her lesbian lifestyle, whereas I was (and often still am) of the opinion that they did not deserve to know much about me. After all, for years they lived very well with a false picture of me and, apart from that, they never showed much interest in seeing anything about me other than that which they wanted to see.

When Christiane made contact with a lesbian self-help group in Berlin, Lesbentreff und Auskunft (LESTRA, or "lesbian meetings and information"), she urged me to join her in the group. I eventually did, although I certainly did not find it easy to follow my sister. I saw, however, that I needed this contact with other lesbians. That was in 1982. And I recognized that, without my sister, it would have taken me far longer to make this step.

Christiane and I worked together for the first time on a project at LESTRA. She had, yet again, found familial connections among the lesbians; I was more drawn to the non-familial lesbians who were working on the project. Shortly after I joined, a conflict developed within the group; it soon came to a head and led to division. I believe the conflict came about because one group saw the project as an extension of their personal spheres of interest, whereas the other wanted to retain openness to the outside world. The conflict ended with one group (those with the familial contact) leaving. The others, including me, carried on with the project. Once again, I felt estranged from my sister and we had little contact with each other for several years.

Since the death of our mother in 1989, something new has slowly developed in my relationship with Christiane. I do not know exactly where we are going — only that we no longer always follow the old paths. She once again means something to me, after I had inwardly rejected her for a long time. The old pain still recurs, and I ask myself: What have they done to us? What have I done to her? What has she done to me?

This year I will be forty. I spent twenty years living inside my family, and I have spent almost another twenty years trying to live my own life. The marks my family left with me are deep. I have had to learn a lot of things, including how to open my mouth and speak. I am still very good at being silent but, in contrast to earlier times, I now have a choice: I can choose silence or speech.

Several times I have broken through my strongly developed loner tendencies — not always with good grace — and have discovered that it can be helpful to make friends with others. I realize that I cannot know in advance whether or not I will be disappointed by the other person. Again, I realize that I have a choice: to be alone or to be with others. There is no guarantee of success, but if I don't try, I will gain nothing at all. So, occasionally, I do jump over my shadow and my fears. It was Christiane who found out about this book project and had the idea that we might participate in it. I do not want to refuse her yet again — my sister, Christiane.

Left: Karin   Right: Christiane

Christiane

The birth-order dynamics in our family are *very* dynamic. I was very much the younger sister, which meant that there was a lot I did not know, but that I also possessed the raw energy to want to overcome that deficit. The fact that I am slightly taller than my sister is not the beginning, or the end, of the competition between us.

The structure within our family is also important — my mother's family was the one that called the tune, was the most popular and set the standards. My grandfather had come to Berlin from Latvia, and my grandmother from Poland, and the family they created here stuck together — or, to put it another way, was held together by irresistible bonds. Family had to be more important than anything else. My father's family, on the other hand, was unpopular: German and uninteresting. Physically, I resembled — and therefore belonged to — my mother's family, the Belewskys (and how proud I was of that). Karin was a Hergl.

As a Belewsky, I had to behave myself, which I did: I was always ready to help and was kind and moderate to my grandparents, aunts (my mother had five sisters and one brother) and cousins. I smiled in the family group photographs and, above all, I was present at the numerous family meetings. I belonged and Karin did not. I could not stop myself from playing the clown for my extended family, because I felt that I was so popular with them — a situation which contrasted starkly to the feelings I had about my place within my own small, immediate family.

So, my feelings about Karin were difficult from the beginning. Above all, we were actually enemies. We each had our own interests, our own girlfriends. I can still remember how surprised my classmates were when they learned that Karin was my sister (she was at the same school, one year ahead of us) because we did not let it be known that we were related. Besides, Karin was often cross with me when I wanted something from her at school, so we had contact with each other there only in exceptional circumstances. Cross and loud-mouthed — that's how I remember her for long stretches of our childhood relationship. And I felt that she was not in solidarity with me, which I took very badly. My father often hit and beat me, and neither my mother nor my sister came to my aid.

We were divided and separate. Once, during an argument, I said to Karin: "You are not my sister any longer" (for a long time before this, I had thought about saying something really mean to her). We argued and quarrelled so much. Once she hit my hand with a stone and, ever since then, one of my fingers has been slightly bent. I hit her when I felt like it; I was stronger and less reserved. Karin would then tell on me, whereupon my father would beat me.

The only thing that we shared was a special liking for our aunt Sonja, who lived in Bremen, alone and independent, and went to work and earned her own money. That is how we also wanted to live: alone and independently, without children. Our aunt Inge in Berlin also lived alone, but she had three illegitimate children, which was a stigma in the 1960s. Her situation was particularly difficult because her third child was fathered by a coloured man, and, because the baby was dark-skinned, my grandfather insisted that it be given up for adoption after the birth. (From then on, I no longer liked my grandfather.) My father, too, was always mean, provocative, condescending and contemptuous toward Inge, whereas he respected Sonja and was polite to her. He also never hit me in front of Sonja, whereas he did not worry about doing so in the presence of others. Sonja really was our shining example. Yet Karin and I even competed for Sonja's affection, and she had to be very careful to write us exactly the same number of postcards.

By the 1980s I was alone, living life as it came, without maintaining contact with my family (I deliberately did not have a telephone). Karin and I both lived in Berlin — we have always lived there and have never been more than fifteen minutes on foot away from each other — and we had both begun to study. She studied law, while I immersed myself in town and regional planning. Karin became so serious about her law studies that meetings with her were always extremely tense. She had a certain manner that did not allow us to talk about some things — however mundane or unimportant — without her feeling insulted. I found always having to behave moderately a form of constant pressure. I had to dance around her on tiptoe just to please her. I began to feel that she had no right to blackmail me into such behaviour.

Like before, each of us had her own friends and interests. I played volleyball and studied, and she studied and was involved with a man. And, like before, I enjoyed it when girls who became my friends found Karin completely different from, and far less nice than, me.

Both of us came out without talking to, or helping, each other. During this time of doubt and fear of rejection, each of us was alone and coping with unavoidable bouts of lovesickness. What we had in common was our political commitment to a left-wing women's group. We took part in demonstrations for the peace movement and squatting rights, and collected signatures. Our mother was proud of us, and often visited us on these campaigns and took photos of us. However, we did not talk to her or to each other about our feelings.

Then, one day, we both found that we had had enough of falling in love with heterosexual women; we discovered that we both wanted, at last, to meet some real lesbians. One afternoon, Karin opened the local newspaper and found an advertisement that read: "Seeking contact with lesbians — clothed or naked." A box number was attached. Well! We agreed that this was just the right thing for us (later, we found out that nobody else had had the nerve to answer this advertisement). And that is how we met our friend Inge and all the women who belonged to her circle.

Suddenly, everyone found it wonderful that Karin and I were sisters: "Lesbian sisters — that must be great," they said. I did not find it at all wonderful. Everyone else did things with their lovers, but I hung out with my sister. How boring. Some people even asked if we had loving feelings for each other — they really had no idea! Meanwhile, Karin fell in love with Inge, who already had a lover. I thought this was very heartless of Karin and saw her as always trying to push herself to the front — as if she was not already ahead of me in certain things! After all, she had already been to bed with women, whereas I had never had a sexual relationship. I longed for one and trembled and shook with insecurity about it. Eventually, though, I did exactly the same thing she had: From the circle of lesbian couples that we knew, I chose one with whom I committed adultery and, afterwards, wanted to go out with — Sonja, my aunt's namesake.

When I could no longer hide the fact that I was a lesbian, I came out to my parents in writing, but I did not have the courage to tell them to their faces. When my mother received my letter, she immediately telephoned me — I had installed a telephone in the meantime — and said she wanted to meet with me. When we got together, she took this opportunity to tell me that, once, a woman — a colleague — had fallen in love with her (my mother was such a beautiful woman), but that she had known she did not want "that." This had happened when I was twelve or thirteen years old, and for the next couple of years, every time the new telephone directories were issued, my mother would phone this woman, only to hang up immediately when she heard her voice. I watched my mother in fascination as she told me this; I did not understand why she had not spoken to the woman.

Through my knowing and belonging to a circle of lesbians, some of my attitudes changed: whereas, previously, I had not liked talking about the fact that I had not had any relationships (after all, I was twenty-five years old), now it was suddenly great that I had never been with a man. In this respect, I had an advantage over Karin. I was one of that rare breed of "original lesbians." At the same time, my relationship with Sonja turned out to be permanent, whereas Karin was "only" having an affair with Inge. That did me good — even if it was unfeminist and reactionary thinking.

With Sonja, I started work on a lesbian project in Berlin. We met twice a week in a café, and suddenly I knew a lot of lesbians and was right in the middle of the scene. After a few months, another batch of lesbians joined us on the project — and one of them was my sister. Once again, everyone was astonished that Karin was my sister, especially since one of the other women looked far more like me and was sometimes even taken to be me. I immediately liked that.

Soon there were twelve women working on the project and, inevitably, we argued. First, we forced someone to leave, and then we got into such a heated debate about another person that the project was split into two camps. Of course, Karin and I were in different camps and it went so far that the faction to which I belonged was edged out — or, rather, we did not want to work under those conditions any longer. For a long time, that was the end of any mutuality between Karin and me. And I did not want it, anyway.

For three years around this time, I did not speak a word to my father. I did not visit him even when he was lying in hospital after his third heart attack. Karin did visit him, and I felt superior to her. We must have had brief contact with each other during this time, but I can't remember much about it. It just did not matter to me. And then … And then our mother died.

I remember visiting her as she was lying in the hospital with a brain tumour. I could see that she was getting more and more strange — so far removed from the person I knew. I felt so helpless. I rushed home and angrily phoned my father and Karin to say that nobody was taking care of her, that no one would tell us what the problem was. Karin was so alarmed that she drove to the hospital the next day and made the doctors examine my mother. And suddenly it was clear that she was going to die.

With the death of my mother, I felt like I had suddenly lost my family. Without her, my contact with my surviving aunts felt barren; and in the year that followed, I had hardly any contact with Karin. On the first anniversary of my mother's death, I went to visit my mother's grave for the first time since she had been buried. As I was standing there, I noticed that there was still was no gravestone over the grave. In a rage, I found my father and took him to task. There was an argument and he hit me. Suddenly, all my inhibitions fell away; I beat him up (later I heard that he had suffered a black eye). Then, trembling, I drove to Karin's home and immediately told her everything. She, too, was furious at my father and took a postcard he had sent her, tore it up and threw it into the rubbish bin. I think that was when we really began learning how to be sisters.

Karin and I are family — and that is exactly what we were both reluctant to admit. We have always lived so near to each other that we can each pop around the corner to the other one's home for a quick coffee. Yet, for a long time, we rarely spoke affectionately to each other; if we did, it was by chance and never deliberate. The hostile way in which we have treated each other would have made any friend flee, and, at some stage, we stopped arguing in front of friends — judging by the shocked expressions on their faces, we appear to be monsters when we fight. Recently, though, we have often laughed when we are alone together. When we have to argue, we get it over and done with as soon as possible. Yet, the question still remains: When will I finally stop reacting so irritably to the same old situations?

For the most part, though, the trouble with the family is over. Karin and I have hardly any contact with our relations in Berlin, although Karin occasionally does visit our father. She and I have became family to each other: a Belewsky and a Hergl have made peace.

Left: Christiane   Right: Karin

Lori Yetman
and Julie Yetman

Left: Lori   Right: Julie

Peanut Butter
and Jam

Lori

There are only six years between my younger sister and me. As an infant, she was beautiful. I loved to hold her tiny body when she was freshly bathed and dressed in soft flannel. I read her poems and nursery rhymes, and sang to her daily after school. I wanted to protect her, shelter her — a desire that has never really dissipated and has probably led to the few conflicts that we have experienced. My baby sister was born at a time when my parents' marriage was at its worst, when our living space was at its smallest, and at a time when I believed that I could fix the very atmosphere in which she so innocently existed. I'm now thirty-two and I'm still holding on to that belief.

After surviving a destructive relationship, I have moved home. In order to regain my strength and to nurture my soul, I needed the unconditional love of my family. I live with my lesbian mother and her lover, while my sister resides in Mom's basement apartment with her lover. When we are peacefully cohabiting, we jokingly refer to our home as "the lesbian commune." However, each of us, at different times, has expressed the need for a separate living space. As one who protects and attempts to fix, it is time for me to move on.

My desire to perfect my mother's and sister's lives, living arrangements, relationships and finances has created some conflict. I have discovered that, although we love one another, there is no way, right now, to synchronize our selves, our relationships and our lives so that all of our dreams for one another are immediately achievable. I had envisioned a three-apartment home where we could care for one another as others come and go. This vision, however, is premature.

Sharing one's sexual identity with one's mother and sister is the norm if one is heterosexual. This is not the case if one is lesbian and living in St. John's, Newfoundland. As far as I know, we are truly unique. We thus tend to be fairly conspicuous as the three of us, with or without our respective lovers, enter the gay bar or the bimonthly women's dance. I have heard various kinds of comments, ranging from "Here comes the cute family" to "Do I have to get your mother's permission to dance with you?" Many people have commented on how lucky I am to have such close, supportive family connections, while others have been more interested in using my insider's knowledge to gain easier access to my sister or mother. After a night downtown, we share stories.

My mother came out to me when I was nineteen. Prior to that moment, I had thought of her as having cultivated friendships with a lot of different women. I did not notice the lack of men at the few parties I had inadvertently crashed. Nor did I question my mother's sexuality when my sister slammed the door in the face of a man wearing a lumber jacket and Kodiacs — and the "man" turned out to be a female friend of our mother. I failed to recognize the obvious because I lacked the conceptual framework — my brain had not been fed the information that women could love women and that these women were "called" lesbians. So when Mom revealed this Truth, my brain was extremely grateful — as was my body. They had both been malnourished. Very gradually, my associations with men diminished and my heterosexual lifestyle lost its already small appeal. I grew closer to my mother, to her lesbian connections and to her way of living. I eventually embraced lesbian identity as my own. And it made sense.

My sister and I had lived similar but separate lives as "straight" women. Our six-year age difference was exacerbated by our heterosexuality. Straight social activity seems to be structured so that age- and class-appropriate behaviour is encouraged. So, while I hung out on campus and frequented a blues bar with other university students, she went to house parties and participated in coed camping trips. We acted appropriately in our respective roles as undergraduate and high-school student.

I was living alone in a small community outside of the city when I came out to Julie. She had temporarily abandoned her boyfriend in order to spend the evening with me. We were discussing her babyhood, our childhood, and our parents' marriage and eventual divorce. Various truths were being revealed and it was thus natural for me to share with her the direction that my life was taking — and the direction that Mom's life had already taken. For the first time, I painfully disclosed that I had been an extremely good actress for years — that I had not been relating to men, emotionally or sexually, in an honest manner and that I had not known this until recently. My acting abilities had been so refined that Julie was surprised. Also, like most children, she could not initially conceptualize Mom as being sexual — especially with the woman we had known as simply "Mom's best friend." Yet she empathized, understood and accepted without question.

Shortly afterwards, from the vantage point of the living-room couch, Julie and her boyfriend would witness me and Mom getting dressed in our coolest of clothes and going out. As we were both single and it was summertime, this occurred often. Julie was asked to join us on most occasions, and I could see her struggling with both her desire to participate in our lives and her loyalty to an increasingly controlling boyfriend. Her desire and his possessiveness eventually led to rebellion. She dumped her boyfriend, permanently, in order to attend a potluck!

The first time that I shared my bed at home with a woman, Julie entered my room the next morning. After a quick warning knock, she opened the bedroom door — and immediately began to apologize when she spotted the two of us sitting up in bed. She was wearing a white terrycloth robe and her hair was long and softly curled. My friend said a very enthusiastic hello to my sister and, as Julie quickly exited, asked even more enthusiastically, "Who was *that*?" I replied, rather sternly, that that was *my* sister and that she was *straight*. It was the first time that I realized that my female lovers, like the men with whom I'd been involved, would also appreciate my sister's beauty. I remember felling something like jealousy on that occasion. But rather than resent Julie for her beauty, I felt disappointed by what I had perceived as my friend's tactlessness. Interestingly, my friend had glimpsed what I had not and questioned my conviction that my sister was straight.

As Julie participated more regularly in my daily activities, our lives began to intertwine on all levels. She would spend time with my lover and me as we played pool in the rec room or went dancing at the bar. When my girlfriend and I would hint at a desire for privacy in order to sexually indulge, the ease with which Julie accepted our lives was evident in the jokes that she'd make. She would wiggle her index finger and laughingly ask if this was how we did it.

I began to learn about individuals within the lesbian community through the often exaggerated horror stories told to me by my lover, and I would worry as these women of "ill repute" questioned me about Julie's sexuality — or, even worse, hit on her. As Big Sister, I was experiencing major anxiety. Unfortunately, my lover and I began to lecture her about "appropriate" lesbian cruising activity and to warn her about women whom she should supposedly avoid. As a result, Julie went underground with her coming-out process and thus began to associate with lesbians outside of our circle. In retrospect, I can see that Mom had done the same thing to me and that, like Julie, I had rebelled. Mom was the protector of her daughters, while I was the protector of my younger sister.

Julie's first relationship is her present one. Mom and I, on the other hand, have experienced a few. Recently, Julie and I discussed the stress that she sometimes experiences when she thinks that her lover may be acting in such a way as to elicit my disapproval. And I realized how much we all try to hide the less desirable traits of our lovers in order to ensure that we all like one another, all of the time. We do not want our bond threatened by normal occurrences such as debates, disagreements or arguments. Julie and I vacation, camp, drink, dance and talk together — we even have a common illness, Crohn's disease. So, if one of us disapproves of aspects of the other's relationship, the very fabric of our existence seems threatened. I had kept things from Julie about my past relationship because I had feared that it would lead to less contact with her. If, for example, I revealed that my lover was treating me badly, I felt that Julie would not join us at the dance. I would thus suppress my need to talk about the problem in order to ensure that she would tolerate my lover's presence and that I could be peacefully in her company. This phenomenon must be incredibly difficult for our lovers. They have to gain not only our respect and love but also our family's. It has not been uncommon for our lovers to express jealousy about our bond.

As children, Julie and I experienced different relationships with our parents. I had been close to both Mom and Dad until the age of six. At that time, my father was increasingly absent because of his career — and, when he was home, the arguing between him and my mother was constant. I thus developed a strong allegiance with my mother, while Julie grew closer to Dad. He would whisk her away to the yacht club or to his workplace, leaving the inevitable argument unresolved. I would thus perceive myself as picking up the broken pieces at home and as being the nurturer of my mother. I had chosen a side — and it was Mom's. At the time, I wondered why Julie had chosen the "wrong" side. And, with my ten-year-old wisdom, I determined that she was just too young to understand. Julie's connection with our father was therefore forgivable.

It has taken me a long time to "forgive" my father for his real and imagined sins. We have developed an unusual relationship over the past ten years — one where our personal lives are never discussed. Instead, we debate issues, reminisce about the more positive aspects of my and Julie's childhoods, or discuss my academic achievements and progress at work. We tend to give each other shy glances and bashful hugs. He invites us to dinner on a weekly basis and cooks us spectacular meals and desserts. His gifts are thoughtful and extravagant, and we know that we could count on his support in a crisis. But does he know about his daughters and ex-wife? We do not know.

Unlike me, Julie gradually incorporated her lover into her relationship with Dad. She has not revealed the nature of their connection but manages to casually refer to the "friendship" in her conversations with Dad. Julie's lover has also stopped hiding in the bedroom on the rare occasions when Dad visits. For reasons that I have not yet determined, I want Dad's approval. I thus concentrate on illustrating my talents and my successes. Because my past relationships were unsuccessful, it never became necessary to share them with Dad. I never felt loved enough or proud enough to risk the exposure and the possible rejection. This may change in the near future, when the woman with whom I want to grow old returns from college in the United States. I will deal with that as it unfolds.

In the meantime, Julie and I continue to ask ourselves: Doesn't he wonder why we never mention dates or boyfriends? Doesn't he question the fact that we have only women friends? Didn't he see the various women who have resided in and then moved from his former home? Doesn't he notice that we frequent a bar we never name? Doesn't he notice that our hair is short, that our clutches are tasteless and that pumps are not part of our wardrobe? Our lesbian existence is becoming increasingly difficult to hide. I am out to everyone except my father, and Julie is not far behind; yet, with him, we have engaged in active deception.

Dad sees us as single sisters who will thus share Christmas Day with each other and Mom. There was one Christmas when Mom was working and Dad was worried that Julie and I would be eating a massive traditional dinner for two. We reassured him in loud, convincing voices that we were cool with this arrangement and that we would be visiting Mom at her workplace. In fact, Julie was driving to her lover's home community on Christmas Eve and returning to eat Christmas dinner with me and my lover. We thus plotted to avoid the telephone until her 2:00 p.m. arrival time so that I would not have to explain her absence from our home on this important family day. A snowstorm delayed Julie's arrival by approximately five hours. During those five hours, I circumvented the telephone and doorbell. Dad had been awaiting his Christmas telephone call — the one in which my sister and I would thank him for his gifts and express our love — and he was worried. I could not respond to his calls because our plan had been to open our gifts together at 2:00 p.m. The story that we fabricated was elaborate, and our Christmas was shadowed by feelings of guilt and remorse. That was two years ago. We have not engaged in such active deception since then. We have told ourselves that he must know, that he is probably too absorbed in his own guilt to initiate the conversation that would reveal the truth. I wonder who we are protecting — Dad or ourselves?

Julie and I need our relationship. Society is generally unaccepting of and, at times, hostile to lesbians. When we came out, we had imagined a lesbian utopia — a community in which women truly loved all aspects of all women and where sexism did not exist. As an undergraduate student, I merged radical feminism with women's stories to describe heterosexuality as an institution that was maintained by the way men have sex. Julie became a Women's Studies graduate as well. Naïvely, we entered the lesbian community believing that masculinity in its negative form would not directly impact on us any longer. Naïvely, we believed that our philosophies would be embraced and that our uniqueness as individuals would be fostered. No such luck. Heterosexual doctrine had infiltrated the lesbian community as well. My first lover believed that feminism was a dirty word. My second lover was probably more sexist than any man I ever encountered. I quickly grew agitated with the femme/blonde jokes that characterized the conversations of most social gatherings. What was most disappointing, however, was the level of conformity necessary to be a member of the lesbian feminist community. Julie and I felt that we had to politically defend every quirky aspect of our personality and lifestyle. So, in order to constructively cope with a very fragmented community, we have created a family of blood ties and love ties. It is our sanctuary — possibly the only place in the world where we can be ourselves and receive unconditional love.

In writing about myself and my sister, I have rediscovered the massive significance of our bond and why we thus feel so threatened by real or potential conflict. If we begin to look at conflict as an event that inspires growth, and if we continue to treat our relationship as something truly precious, I know that Julie and I will be sisters — in every sense of the word — for life.

Julie

Lori is my older and somewhat wiser sister. We are many people to each other, but, most important, we are friends. I think this is what makes our relationship so special; it may also make it more complicated. For instance, sometimes I think we are too close and know too much of every aspect of each other's lives. If there is an aspect of her life that I don't like, I feel a need to help her change it, or even better it. Many sisters want the best in life for each other and may try to initiate change in the other's life, even if that change is premature. If I know Lori is unhappy in a particular situation, my desire is to eradicate the problems and restore her happiness.

We try not to interfere too much in each other's relationships with our respective lovers, but, at times, opinions — good and bad — are freely shared. I have been with my soulmate, Sandi, for over seven years, and if we have an argument and Lori hears about it, Sandi gets the cold shoulder not only from me, but from Lori as well. It's a difficult predicament for Sandi — living with her lover and her lover's mother and sister, whoare all trying to protect one another from real or imaginary harm. However, our home is a pretty cool place in which to live, once you get past all the bodyguards.

Lori was a love-child. This fact is unabashedly admitted by our mother, Lin, who also claims that she had sex only twice with our father and that Lori and I are the results of those encounters. She tells me my birth was planned so that Lori would be old enough to look after me and, in this way, all the demands involved in raising a child would be shared between the two of them. And it's true that, through the years, I have often said, "Jesus, Lori, you sound just like Mom!" Lori has indeed been like my other mother.

Lori has been a strong influence in my life, especially in the more formative years of adolescence and early adulthood. Her absolute presence in my life has influenced everything, from my tastes in music to my choices of study in university. She may even have influenced my choice of coming out by speeding up the inevitable process. She gave me the courage to be me. For reasons which I sometimes don't fully understand, her opinions regarding my life, my lover, and my very being have been of the utmost importance to me. Sometimes I wish she could just be my sister; it's hellish having two moms. Aren't sisters supposed to watch you grow and make mistakes, give you some advice and hand-me-downs, and then let you go on your merry way? Lori has done all that and more, but I have had the added pressure of her desire to mother me. The downside of this is that she may still see me as a little girl. My character flaw is that I regress easily into being that child who wants nothing more than to appear absolutely good in the eyes of her mothers.

Lori and I have a good relationship, but we do occasionally have fights — probably not as frequently as most other sisters because we try to avoid it. When we are mad at each other, I feel like there is some sort of upset in the balance of nature. I simply can't function normally if I think she's angry with me. When we do fight, Lori reminds me of a cool and collected lawyer, while I'm the frustrated and emotional defendant who cannot compete with her well-thought-out case against me (Lin and I always thought Lori should be a lawyer). More often than not, we resolve our arguments by not resolving them and just forget whatever it was we were fighting about. As is true of most people who are in any type of close relationship, our arguments come out of clashes in personalities and ideas. And even though we have so much common ground between us, we are still very different people.

Left: Lori   Right: Julie

Our parents divorced when I was around eleven years old. Because Lori was older and more aware of the problems that had existed between our parents, for a period of time she drifted away from Dad, while I retained a fairly good weekend relationship with him. We often wonder if Dad has us figured out; if he does, he seems okay with it. He never asks about boyfriends or marriage plans (except to suggest that, if we do get married, we should marry someone rich and let love come later) and I have been brave enough to talk about my lover in his presence as if she were my best friend. We haven't felt the need to come out to him. Yet there are obvious gaps and too many women in our lives, so we believe that he has probably drawn his own conclusions about our sexuality. I don't have a need to put it into words because he seems to accept me as I am without the attached label.

It was during the time of the divorce that my world began to be filled more and more with women. I never questioned my mother about why she had so many female friends or why she invited only women to her parties. I probably just assumed that all these women were divorced and, like my own mother, did not want or need men at this point in their lives. Even when her best friend and her friend's daughter moved into our home, I did not think that Mom was a lesbian. My friends, however, were much more inquisitive. They would ask me why my mother's friend and her daughter were living with us. I would give the standard "sharing expenses" line, which, I found out later, was only a half-truth.

When I finally did learn that Lin, and then Lori, were lesbians, I wasn't very shocked on either occasion. My most basic reaction was that everything made sense: This explained all the short-haired women in their lives. Moreover, I had been questioning my own sexuality for years and did not have to feel so alone in my confusion. In my experience, males were overbearing, selfish and narrow-minded. Lori and Lin had given me crash courses in feminism and taught me that women did not have to be passive and meek. I therefore felt restricted in heterosexual relationships and was getting tired of having heated debates with guys over feminist issues. I felt misunderstood. I did experience a few negative feelings about my mother's and sister's lesbianism, probably because it is difficult in any situation to imagine one's own mother and sister as sexual beings. In this case, my way of coping with this new situation was to jokingly refer to my family as "freaks of nature."

When Lori came out to me, my exposure to the gay world dramatically increased. I was in my late teens and we both realized that our age difference of six years really made no difference. We shared common interests and beliefs, and were rediscovering each other as friends. She started taking me to women's film festivals and dances, and I would occasionally join her and Lin for a night downtown at our one gay bar. This I enjoyed, simply because I was totally fascinated with this newly discovered subculture whose members included my sister, my mother and their friends — some of whom I had known since I was a child. I would stare in amazement at men dancing with men, and the butched-up women for whom Lori held her own fascination at that time.

Like Lori in her coming-out process, I left the safety of my lesbian family in order to seek out my own niche in the gay community. After all, it's difficult to meet people when your sister is in the background glaring and giving the message, "Back off. She's my sister." Even on my own it wasn't much easier, because I felt that people would not take me seriously as a lesbian. I think many people found it hard to believe that we were all gay, and were, therefore, afraid to be involved with someone they thought was merely experimenting. One of the few exceptions was Sandi, whom I met the first night I decided to go to the bar by myself. But even she did not let me forget who I was, with her unique pick-up line: "So, you're Lori's sister. Want to dance?" (I found out later in our relationship that she did not even know Lori personally but thought she would use her name as a sort of reference!)

When I began my relationship with Sandi, I was wary of admitting it to Lori — in fact, I even lied, telling her that we were just friends. At that time, I believed that Lori would not take me seriously either. As well, I was still questioning myself: Was I really a lesbian? Or was I just being influenced by my sister and mother? I wanted to be sure of myself before I made any announcements. Lori was suspicious, went into protection mode, and would get Lin to call me at Sandi's to make sure I was all right. But, thankfully, Lori quickly accepted Sandi and they now laugh, quarrel and protect like sisters themselves.

Lori is my mentor, my pseudo-mother, my prosecuting attorney, my hero and my antagonist. We lead parallel lives, separate yet united in our mutual acknowledgement of the significance and importance of our bond as sisters and as friends.

Louise Fleming
and Lee Fleming

Left: Louise   Right: Lee

Through Thick
and Thin

Louise

Why did we decide to do a book on lesbian sisters? And whose idea was it anyway? Lee will probably say that she came up with the idea, but I'm sure that the idea was mine and Lee enthusiastically supported it.

I wonder: Why did we both want to explore our relationship as lesbian sisters? Do we see it as very different from our relationships with our three other sisters? And, if it is, just what makes it different? Is "different" a polite way of saying "better"? Will our straight sisters feel upset or left out, or will they think that we probably wished they were lesbians too? And our mother — will she read our articles hoping to understand just how she produced two lesbian daughters (or, as I once said to her, two so far)? Perhaps she'll just be proud of our accomplishments, which include editing and publishing this book (although she may ask herself why we had to put our barenaked bodies on the front cover).

And what of our brothers? Will they roll their eyes and ask themselves why we have to keep on exploring our lesbianism or will they make a few jokes about big sister/little sister rivalry? Will they have a deeper understanding of their lesbian sisters?

And our father: if he were alive, would we have told him about this book? Or would we have assumed that the mere fact that it was about his two lesbian daughters meant that he needed to be kept in the dark?

These are the questions that have been on my mind since Lee and I set a date to meet and exchange our first drafts. The relationship I have with Lee has, for the most part, been separate from my relationship with the rest of the family. From time to time, I may share with other family members a glimpse of the trials, tribulations and triumphs of my relationship with Lee, but they all live very far away and we live five minutes apart. My lesbian-sister relationship has been free from censure, except for the self-imposed kind.

I want to begin by saying that I love Lee very deeply — she is an essential part of my life. She has been at my side, rooting for me, when I needed a cheerleader, she has been a phone call away when I needed to fall apart, she has been my best friend when I needed someone to believe in me and she has risked giving me difficult critical feedback when I needed to be smartened up. Without her, my life would be less enriched, less fun and less outrageous. We have grown up together, lived together, holidayed together, worked together, grieved together and occasionally fought together. For a short time, we were even estranged from each other.

Lee is the youngest of my four younger sisters — she's six and a half years younger than me, although most people can't tell (until they get to know us, that is). One of the perks of being the fat, older sister is that wrinkles haven't really cracked my face, while Lee has inherited that well-aged look found on the thin members of our family. Everyone knows that the oldest daughter in a big family usually has lots of responsibilities and that the youngest get lots of attention. That's how it worked in my family — I was my mother's helper from a young age (a role that I liked, I hasten to add), able to take on all kinds of tasks without hesitation. Lee was the cute littlest sister, able to entertain the crowd with her adorable and precocious personality and always land on her feet, no matter how high she jumped.

Of course, neither of us is simply the product of her rank in the family; each of us has travelled down a different path, and our life experiences are very different. I pursued my education for as long as I could and then catapulted onto the corporate ladder of success. I stayed in the heterosexual zone until my late twenties and didn't stop climbing the career path until my late thirties. I believed in change from within the system and enjoyed the big money I earned as a senior manager. The acquisition of material goods and the pleasures of life were important to me — I loved having a nice house, a well-stocked liquor cabinet, good food and money to travel. And I loved sharing my things with my friends. Lee passed on university, travelled in the Caribbean, came out at a young age, did a crash course in accounting and then opened her own business (a women's book-store) in her early twenties. She ran it with much success for five years, then decided to follow her heart and move East.

Although we had both been living in the same town for several years before she moved East, we were caught up in relationships and never seemed to have much time for each other. I knew that I needed a change in my life, and when Lee told me she was planning to move to Prince Edward Island to be with a woman, I decided to look for a job in the same province. I remember that we discussed how much more time we would have for each other if we lived in a smaller place and I also remember thinking that I wouldn't want to live anywhere that Lee didn't. A month after she packed her bags and joined her lover, I moved too. A moving van took my belongs, my car and my pets — and I boarded a plane for Prince Edward Island.

That was over eight years ago.

My life has changed significantly in the last eight years. With the support of Lee and other women, I threw off the shackles of the boys' club, with all its attendant compromises and uncomfortable clothes; left my secure job; bought a publishing house; and, after sowing some wild oats, settled down with a wonderful woman and her young child.

Lee became a much bigger part of my life almost from the moment I arrived on Prince Edward Island. We spent lots of time together. We were both vulnerable and lonely — the relationship that caused her to move to Prince Edward Island changed in ways she hadn't anticipated, and I was finally able to let out my pain from a five-year relationship that had taken its toll on me. So we drowned our sorrows and we also had fun together — enjoying the comforts that my lifestyle afforded, hanging out at the beach, being outra-geous in our small community. We enjoyed being ourselves with each other; many times, it was a relief to be alone with each other because we didn't have to worry about other people's reactions: No guilt about hogging centre stage or speaking a mile a minute or talking *ad nauseam* about our childhoods. We formed a mutual admiration society and could spend hours being totally silly. These days, we still enjoy spending time together when we're alone and can do whatever we want; those times are very rare, however, because neither of us lives alone and we both have families.

On the other hand, because we are both in committed, long-term relationships and because we both really like each other's lover, our lesbian family has expanded. We each have a "dil" (dyke-in-law). Our dils have created new family ties that are uniquely lesbian in nature. Lee has taken an active role as aunt to Sarah, our six-year-old. She takes Sarah overnight one day a week and on the occasional weekend. Over the years, Lee and Sarah have developed a close relationship. Lee loves Sarah and appreciates her uniqueness — perhaps because they are both Librans, they share the desire for perfect harmony. Sarah considers Lee to be part of her immediate family and loves the attention and craziness she gets from her Auntie Leelee, just as long as Lee doesn't embarrass her in public. (Why does this seem so familiar?) For me, watching Lee and Sarah together is recognizing the continuation of our lesbian family into the next generation. Like any proud mother, I think my child is the best in the whole world, and it warms me to share this with my sister.

I sometimes ask myself: What would it be like if one of us weren't a lesbian? Couldn't we still have a close sister relationship? What does our lesbianism add?

I have very close relationships with my other sisters and I don't wish to minimize them; nonetheless, my relationship with Lee encompasses my whole life. We share a community, a culture, a language, a past, values, a sense of humour and an understanding of living in the world as a lesbian. (We make a point of *not* sharing lovers, past or present!) There isn't anything about my life that I couldn't tell Lee.

This doesn't mean that we have a perfect relationship. We have our ups and our downs — as does any intense and close relationship — and perhaps we even have more of them because we are sisters. It's inescapable at times. I will always be Lee's big sister, and she will always be my baby sister. We will probably always struggle with the behaviours that come from our position in the family; sometimes they will be impossible to overcome.

What are those behaviours and how have they/do they affect our lesbian-sister relationship? At times, Lee and I have intertwined our

TO SAPPHO, MY SISTER

lives so closely that it has been impossible to see each other with any objectivity. Lee worked for me at the press for two years, and by the end of that period we were in dire need of a complete break from each other in order to put the balance back in our relationship. I know I walk a fine line between being supportive and helpful to Lee and telling her what to do. I have a strong urge to make things better in Lee's life and, because I've been around longer and have been successful in life, I think I've got the answers for her life. Sometimes Lee just wants my approval, even if she couches the request in different terms. And, sometimes she just wants me to listen. I'm still working on listening ...

What is it that I want from her? Sometimes I wish she'd worry less about life and spend her boundless energy making the important things happen for her. She's still landing on her feet no matter where she jumps from, and there are no signs that this innate skill will weaken; however, she'd be more content — and I'd be off the hook — if she had some of the "things" that seem to mean security and stability in our world. I wouldn't be the only one to have amassed the comforts of life. And I want her to keep on being my best lesbian-sister friend and speaking her mind, even if I can't always acknowledge the truth in what she's saying.

Lee continues to be closely connected to the press — she's our bookkeeper, manuscript second reader and book editor. She's helped renovate our building, pitched in when we needed another pair of hands, represented the press whenever she has the opportunity and unabashedly been our biggest fan. My partner and I respect her judgment and her intuition. Every feminist business could benefit from a Lee.

Surviving in the world as a woman and a lesbian is often a demanding job. Having a lesbian sister can make it easier. If I had a wish for all the lesbians out there, it would be to have a lesbian sister just like Lee.

Back: Louise Front: Lee

Lee

May 28, 1995

It's a sunny spring afternoon. I'm in the living room and the place is blessedly quiet for a change. My mind has been on the theme of lesbian sisters for months. As the editor of this anthology, I've received the outpourings of sisters from many different life situations and family backgrounds. Now it is time for me to get out of my editorial head and into my heart; it is time to write about my life with Louise.

Funny how I've delayed writing my own submission. Now I understand the hesitation of some contributors when they were asked to talk about a relationship that is so personal and intimate, yet taken so much for granted. I want to share our anecdotes; remember the many times we have been there for each other; let go of the hard, unbending times; and ponder our ongoing connection. I want to catch the essence of this bond between us.

My relationship with Louise has had several distinct phases, and the most significant one for me has been the past eight years since we moved to Prince Edward Island together. This last year has been a particularly challenging time of change. With the death of our father last July, we've both been grieving. I have been introverted and protective and emotional. And I have seen these things in Louise as well. We grieve very differently, but there is a complicity in this that those outside our family circle, even our lovers, cannot share.

We're from a big, Catholic family. Mom had seven kids in eight and a half years. First, there was a son; then, Louise; then, a boy, three girls, and, last, me. Louise was always my big sister, the "second mother." I was cared for, tended to and defended by her. When I entered my teens, I loved to observe her as she applied her make-up and put her hair up in curlers. I listened to her music: The Supremes, Gary Lewis & The Playboys, Neil Diamond. I watched her stand up to my father and challenge his socialized stereotypes about the place of girls in the world.

I was the tomboy sister who took pleasure in embarrassing Louise as she went out on her first dates. She was my bossy older sister who seemed to revel in having sister-minions to do her bidding. She tried (in vain) to help me develop study habits and she taught me to skate. I remember walking home from school with her arm through mine, and I knew I was safe and okay with my big sister.

When she finally went off to Toronto to attend university, I was so thrilled when she invited me to come and visit her at her residence. She was a bona fide grown-up. Before then, I had had no concept of Louise as anything more than my big sister. Everything I had felt about her was through the filter of "family."

In 1976, when I was in my last year of high school, Louise went off to France to teach. It was just my parents and me left in the family home. Louise had stored all of her university course books in the basement. These included lots of CanLit, some French-Canadian literature and some feminist texts. The only subject that held my interest throughout high school was English, and I was an avid reader; I started to read through Louise's collection. I'll never forget the afternoon that I was rummaging around and found a copy of *Sappho Was a Right-on Woman*. I was having serious questions about my sexual identity, but had no way to describe what I was feeling. Here was a book that said it all, and in no uncertain words. I hid the book in my shirt and smuggled it up to my bedroom, where I devoured its contents in one sitting. Finding that book was the single most important step in my coming-out process. It is forever linked to Louise. After I absorbed the book's revelations, I started to wonder about Louise. Did this mean that she might be a lesbian? I remember tearing back down to the basement to see if there were any other lesbian books in her boxes, but I came up empty-handed. Then I remembered how, the previous year, she had brought home a friend from university, Alison, who was from Liverpool, England. I had been totally infatuated with Alison. Could she be Louise's girlfriend, and did that then mean Louise was a lesbian? These questions remained unanswered for a long while, as Louise was away and I was too afraid to write and ask her.

Ironically, I came out as a lesbian first. I was twenty-one. Louise was twenty-seven and an avowed heterosexual. I kept telling her that I thought she was a lesbian, but she would retort, "You think *everyone* is a lesbian." Then, one Saturday, after she had been living in another city for about four or five months, she called and said, "Guess what?"

Without missing a beat, I replied, "You've slept with a woman." That woman happened to be a lesbian I had roomed with briefly while she was completing part of her university degree program in Ottawa. Louise came out with Sibyl — a wonderful, proud lesbian — and then they went their separate ways, Sibyl to the Yukon, and Louise eventually back to Ottawa.

Perhaps that is when our power dynamic shifted and when we became peers. I had finally done one thing before Louise had. *She* was the baby dyke, and I the semi-experienced one. As lesbians, we were on an even footing. And the feminist bookstore that I opened in 1982 with my then-partner put me right in the middle of the women's community spotlight. I felt like I had finally grown up, that I had transcended my position as youngest sister. Little did I know that there was a further balance to be struck. To have a truly meaningful, enduring relationship we would both have to work harder than I have worked with some lovers in my life!

And speaking of lovers in our lives: I have had a series of relationships over the years, as has Louise. Neither of us was ever totally comfortable with the other's lovers. I felt that they were always a bit jealous of me, or perhaps they were jealous of my relationship with Louise. I'm not sure. But since Louise has reunited with Sibyl, the woman she came out with back in 1980, and I have also settled into a stable long-term relationship with my partner, Heidi, our lives as lesbians have had the added dimension of sharing time as couples. I also have a relationship separate and apart with

Sibyl, a woman I respect, like and love immensely. Additionally, I have become, over the past five years, an "auntie" to Sibyl and Louise's six-year-old daughter. Louise and Sibyl are, in turn, very generous in their inclusion of Heidi's three children in their lives. Special events like Thanksgiving and Christmas always include our two families getting together.

My five-year relationship with Heidi is the longest I have ever experienced with any woman, and I am becoming more comfortable being part of a "couple" (a term I always despised). There have been so many changes in my life since I met Heidi — and, since there are children involved, the changes seem even more intense and constant. I am still in the process of defining myself within our couple and family, even as my interaction with Louise and her family is evolving.

It has taken more years than Louise knows for me to allow her to be a person unto herself, and not the big sister that I was trying to live up to or stand up to or please. Of all my six relationships with my siblings, my relationship with Louise is the most challenging; I have the most invested in her, as well. I know this has much to do with our physical proximity, and with how much of our social and work lives overlap. All my other brothers and sisters live in another city far from here. It is Louise and I who form "family" away from the others, out here, on the east coast.

I have thought a lot about the relationship that I have with each of my other sisters and compared it with what I have with Louise. I've concluded that there is, in some way, no real basis for comparison. Each sister bond has a life of its own. I have been fortunate to feel so loved, and loving toward, my sisters — all of them. The birth-order dynamic comes into play here, because there is a kind of affinity that I share with my sister Mardi, who is sixteen months my senior. She made me whole by her sheer existence in my life as a child, and that hasn't changed with the years. My sister Jean, who is three years older than me, is also a big part of my childhood story. We were inseparable as kids, and yet we fought tooth and nail. The three of us were designated within the family as "the three little girls" — a unit unto ourselves. My sister Loretta is "the middle child." She was an individual, set apart from us in many ways. I didn't feel particularly connected to her. Recently, that has begun to change and I find I have many things in common with her, especially our mutual artistic involvement and expression.

Louise and I are certainly very different from each other. She is the oldest daughter; I am the youngest. She is the practical, thorough and grounded Taurus; I am the flitting, speedy and idealistic Libran. She demands loyalty, is authoritative, knows her own mind and has assets; I am conciliatory, wired for sound, a worrier and cash-poor. Despite these differences, we appreciate many of the same things in life — the most important being a sense of humour. There are very few women in my life with whom I can have more fun than Louise. We both love food, language, music, women and each other. We are both political, in-your-face dykes. Together we have laughed till we've cried. We have also screamed and raged, and always forgiven each other.

When my partner and I decided to open up Ottawa's first feminist bookstore in 1982, Louise was the first woman in the community to lend us some start-up cash. When her first long-term lesbian relationship ended, I was there through her tears. I have been her fence-builder, house-cleaner and mover, bookkeeper and general handywoman. She has kept me solvent on more than one occasion. When I need good, practical advice on any matter, I always call Louise first. We both agree that we have a mutually beneficial arrangement. We have always been there for each other.

It still is a challenge for me to surmount my "family of origin" stuff with Louise. It becomes easier as the years pass, but our big sister/little sister dynamic still crops up in times of stress. I think I tend to impose that into our relationship more than Louise does. I second-guess Louise, and imagine her disapproval or judgment when it's the last thing on her mind.

She has often been a mirror for me. In social settings, I'll watch her take up a lot of space. She'll be entertaining and engaging, but sometimes there won't be room for others to have their say. And I'll realize that I do the very same thing. At one time that part of Louise used to infuriate me. To paraphrase what someone once said, "What we don't like in others is often what we don't like in ourselves." But one of the good things about me getting older is that I'm more forgiving of myself and others. I also know that I have my hands full in just keeping my own heart and soul together, let alone taking on anyone else's. I've learned to be more accepting of who she is.

When Louise is especially embarrassed or irritated by me (a big-sister dynamic that I seem to elicit from her) she will sometimes say, "Pretend that you've just met me" or "Pretend we don't know each other." It used to hurt my feelings; it was like I was definitely not okay the way I was. I guess it was her way of saying "Let's clear the playing field and not bring our history to this interaction." I am realizing, after all these years, that this is an impossible thing to do. We can let go of the parts of our past that are no longer useful, but we will always be sisters. We grew up in the same house, with the same parents and value system. It is the glue that has held us together through our individual relationship break-ups, through the new careers and new partners, through the process of aging and, most recently, through the death of our father and our shared family grief.

I'm experiencing my world so differently now than I did in my early thirties, in my twenties and in my childhood. Louise and I have been re-establishing a healthier connection as peers after my two-year stint in her company as her employee. Working for her had many good points, but we both now know that certain boundaries, especially around power dynamics, are healthy to have in place. Her being my boss is just too much of an old, not-so-good family dynamic for me. Since I've left her employ, we've re-established a healthier, more egalitarian relationship.

With the return of summer, and its heat, I feel myself whole again. I feel my connection to this earth, to my community, to my lover and my family. Louise and I have laughed and cried our way to a mature and intentional relationship as lesbian sisters. It feels so complex and full of winding side roads. I wish the two of us could sit up all night with a video camera and capture our stories — the uncensored, hilarious ones; the sad and angry ones. We are forever sisters; but, beyond this, we are lesbian sisters. We can count on each other in a way that only family can — through thick and thin — and we *choose* to have each other in our lives in such an intentional way.

It's hours later and I'm still sitting in the living room. I'm now putting myself through my daily classical guitar practice. The phone rings; it's Louise. We have one of our quick "touch base" calls. It could be about a hundred things — her business, the kids, our family, plans for the weekend. After I get off the phone, I sit looking out the window, contemplating the new growth on the trees outside. I realize just how much I love this sister of mine, with a sturdy, everyday, forever, proud kind of love. It has stood the fire of time and estrangement, and moved to reconciliation and acceptance. This love has not always been easily expressed or lived out between the two of us. But in this little existential moment, there it is: that essence that I've so wanted to catch.

Biographical Notes

Jan Andrews lives on Lily Creek Farm just outside of Ottawa with Colleen, her partner of nine years. She is a counsellor at a community health centre, working to end violence against women. Her body and heart are growing stronger as she gardens, plays with the horses, repairs the barn and fences, watches the birds at the feeder and becomes ever more conscious of nature's beauty and magic.

Lynn Andrews is a writer, artist and lucky sister living in eastern Ontario. She lives with her partner, Sandy, Sandy's son, Aidan, and a number of wise animal friends.

Diana Andrews was born in Toronto in the fall of 1960 and has lived there all her life. A strong sense of self, coupled with an independent nature, led her to pursue ambitions beyond the societal limitations of her multi-racial, lower-working-class roots. She has a degree in French Language and Literature, is co-chair of her Masters' Swim Club, and holds the position of instructor-trainer with the Canadian Royal Lifesaving Society.

Wendy Baxter is a fine artist with a Masters of Social Work. She lives in Santa Cruz, California, with her partner and daughter. She works for the Santa Cruz AIDS Project.

Janet Bianic, forty-six, is a former Albertan who is now living in Vancouver, B.C. She finds comfort in native Indian spirituality, and makes rawhide drums, rattles and masks. She is also a poet and a consultant who works with groups on community change. Since she and her sister found one another again five years ago, they are creating a new sense of family and learning that sisterhood goes deeper than blood and bone.

Eva Borgström is forty years old. She lives alone but has a girlfriend, joint custody of a cat, and a house in the countryside from a previous relationship. She has a Ph.D. and does research and teaches in a women's studies department. She also makes music in her free time.

Gunnel Borgström is twenty-eight years old. Like her sister, she lives alone but has a girlfriend. She works as a process engineer/laboratory worker at a water purifying plant. She also coaches table tennis and enjoys exercising, nature, and life in general.

Carol Camper is a writer, editor, visual artist and women's health worker. A Black lesbian born in Toronto, Carol's multi-racial ancestry also includes Native North American and European roots. Her most recent project, the anthology *Miscegenation Blues: Voices of Mixed Race Women*, was published by SisterVision Press (1994) and is in its second printing.

Gillean Chase, forty-nine, is the author of *Triad Moon* (gynergy books), and two volumes of poetry, *The Distress of Harvest* (Fiddlehead Press) and *The Square Root of Female* (Ragweed Press). She shares with her sister, Janet, a strong interest in poetry and in wiccan spirituality. She has worked as a teacher of highschool English, and has been an arts administrator, counsellor, fundraiser and community advocate. She loves gardening and the work of building intimate relationships.

Anne and Theresa Corrigan have known each other for forty-one years. Theresa had the opportunity to be an only child for five years; Anne does not ever want that opportunity. Both live in California — Anne in San Diego and Theresa in Sacramento. Anne is a research scientist, stained glass artist and landscape designer who lives with ten cats. Theresa, who lives with three dogs and seven cats, is a writer, a Women's Studies teacher and the owner of Lioness Books, a feminist bookstore. We loved working on this article together and it did not prompt one fight.

Alix Dobkin is in the process of writing her memoirs after twenty years spent on the road, visiting and singing for Lesbian communities all over the English-speaking world. She has had the unique privilege of helping to lay the foundation for a rich and thriving Lesbian culture. Her sixth album, *Love and Politics*, is a twenty-song compilation that summarizes thirty years of writing and entertaining. Her first album, *Lavender Jane Loves Women*, was produced in 1973 with Kay Gardner, and holds the distinction of being the first internationally distributed Lesbian album.

Julie Ann Dobkin was born in New York City in 1949 and was raised (for the most part) in Philadelphia as an expatriate New Yorker. After some college in Madison, Wisconsin, and some art school in Manhattan, she messed around, worked and lived in Boston from 1975 to 1981. It was there that Julie experienced her first serious relationship with a woman. She came out in 1980. A year later, she left for San Francisco to study massage and healing. Julie has been a massage therapist for more than thirteen years, and is happily sustained by her practice. She is an active member of Voices: Bay Area Lesbian Choral Ensemble. She and her lover live in Oakland with Kekoa, their revered canine crone.

Lee Fleming is, at the age of thirty-seven, moving closer to her heart's desire — playing music full-time. She has also made some films and videos, done a bit of writing and interviewing, and edited two other anthologies for gynergy books (*By Word of Mouth: Lesbians Write the Erotic* and *Tidelines: Stories of Change by Lesbians*).

Louise Fleming is a forty-four year old Taurean business woman who delights in making people laugh. Her life is very full — when she's not travelling, baking up a storm, floating in the ocean, or spending time with her lover and their daughter, she's hard at work finding ways to make a lesbian publishing house both viable and fun. She looks forward to early retirement, proof that she's still a dreamer at heart.

Barbara Grier was born in Cincinnati, Ohio, on November 4, 1933. A lifelong activist in the lesbian/gay movement, she worked at all manner of odd clerical and service jobs — as a car hop, office clerk, secretary, collector and skip tracer — at the same time as she collected lesbian literature and worked for lesbian magazines (*The Ladder*, in particular). In 1973, she and Donna J. McBride, her lover of twenty-three years, founded a lesbian publishing company, The Naiad Press, Inc. Today, Barbara and Donna live northwest of Tallahassee, Florida, in a pine forest.

Diane Grier was born in Detroit, Michigan, on July 6, 1939, and grew up in the mid-west United States. She received a combined B.Sc./B.A. degree in 1961, from Central Missouri State University. After working in research and investments for thirty years, she is now happily retired and living in the country outside of Joplin, Missouri, with Geyne Kent, her lover of thirty-three years.

Karin Hergl was born in Berlin in 1955, with her sun in Taurus. She loves money, independence and hot babes.

Christiane Hergl lives on earth, loves women and works.

Gail Hewison teaches and practices yoga, studies watercolour painting and has exhibited three times, lives with her partner Liz, who is a doctor, loves being by the sea, writes book reviews and tries to live a day at a time.

Catherine Hughes is a farmer, an artist and an activist. She is white and grew up middle class, mostly in Kingston, Ontario, but also in the United States and in Nairobi, Kenya. Her parents, Margaret and Ian Hughes, are a potter and a mathematics professor, respectively. She has a lesbian sister, Mikaela, and a brother, Daniel, who is a painter. She lives on a dairy farm in Pictou County, Nova Scotia, with her compañera, Jane Morrigan, and their foster daughter, Jacques Pierre Besancon.

Mikaela Hughes is a temporarily unemployed "Intern Architect." She has recently completed an M.Phil. in Environment and Energy Studies in Architecture. Her life over the past few years has involved many changes in living arrangements and relationships. Two constants have been karate (she is a Shodan in Shotokan) and soccer, which is her social life (let's go Amazons!).

Caffyn Kelley is editor and publisher at Gallerie Publications, where she has produced numerous books by women artists. She is a fabric artist and a writer. She lives in a rural area near Vancouver, accessible only by boat.

Joy McBride lives in Kingston, Ontario with her two cats, Rory and Ohio. She likes to coach soccer, walk by the lake and bake for friends.

Karen McBride and her partner live in Guelph, Ontario. Karen makes her living as a computer programmer but her real passions are woodworking, her old house, her VW van and her black lab, Murphy.

Anne-Marie Pedler spent her early childhood in South Australia, on a farm and at a Catholic boarding school. She worked as a primary school teacher for seven years, then moved into teacher training for seven years, focusing on women, educational research and designing school programs for girls. She gradually moved into the lesbian community as a magazine writer and now talks, shares ideas and partakes in mutual inspiration over books in her feminist bookshop at the seaside. She lives with her favourite lesbians: Jeannie, a nine-year-old spaniel; Sister Cat; and Cocoa, the tortoise shell minder. What she really wants to do is be on the stage.

Robyn Pedler — Sagittarian, thirty-eight, photographer — loves a "bushie" (campfire) out in the backyard as she dances with her cat, CatWomin, and knits.

Yvette Perreault is the eldest child in a large, Prairie-rooted francophone family. She has been living in Toronto since '82 and, after a decade of AIDS activism, she now co-ordinates a provincial project responding to the bereavement needs of front-line AIDS workers. Her focus on both personal and community loss has lead to her interest in quantum physics and chaos theory as principles for community transformation.

Suzanne Perreault is part of the west coast branch of the Perreault family. She and two close friends have recently bought a house in Vancouver's east end. Suz works with a provincial group advocating for seniors, and she cherishes her elderly but still lively cat, Ouija. Currently on an inward journey of self-exploration, Suz is discovering tender parts of her old/new self.

Gisele Perreault is part of the United States contingent of the Perreault clan. She lives and works in Chicago as an artist. Her creations include extraordinary masks and unique stained glass pieces. She shares a home with her partner and four lovely cats, two of whom are huge, hairy Maine-Coons.

Libby Silva learns ballroom and belly dancing (with lesbians of course), plays bridge, loves to travel, meditates, writes poetry, knits fabulous things and keeps bees.

Eva Steck was born in Stuttgart, Germany in November 1967. She grew up in the United States and in different parts of Germany. After high school she trained for three years and became a professional gardener. After this apprenticeship, she studied pedagogy in Göttingen. She received her diploma in 1993. Today she works in a shop for agricultural supplies and organic food, located in an old mill close to Göttingen. She is training to become a therapeutic riding teacher. Her hobbies include music, literature and martial arts, and she spends a lot of energy on political and cultural projects for women and lesbians.

Ursula Steck was born in Stuttgart, Germany in September 1964. She grew up in the United States and different parts of Germany. After high school she worked on a farm for one year and then went to Cologne to study English literature and linguistics, philosophy and library science. She finished her studies with a thesis on non-verbal communication in the novels of Margaret Laurence. She received her M.A. in 1991. Today she works as an editorial assistant for the German Journal of Air and Space Law and as a freelance creative writer and journalist. Her work also includes PR jobs for different women artists. Her hobbies are music, netsurfing and books, books, books.

Jane Waddy is a psychologist, lectures in child-protection, loves gardening, is studying watercolour painting (with success similar to that of her sister, Gail Hewison), goes power walking, and lives with her partner, Jan, a university lecturer. They do aquarobics together at the local pool every morning at 6 a.m., summer and winter!

Sändra Washington is thirty-five years old, was born and raised in Columbus, Ohio, and spent an inordinate amount of time reading books and fantasizing about the perfect life. In addition, she went to school, got jobs, found many *good* friends and a few lovers. By the time she moved to Lincoln, Nebraska, Sändra had a master's degree in Natural Resources, a performance career with The Washington Sisters and a lot of ideas about gardening, cooking and flower arranging. Sändra works as a community/park planner for the United States National Park Service. Her greatest joy is building a life with her partner.

Dr. Sharon J. Washington is an educator, performer and consultant committed to social change. She brings to her work a strong identity as a woman, an African American with indigenous roots, a feminist and a lesbian. She received her Ph.D. from Ohio State University, where she completed a dual major in Adventure Education and Leisure Management, with a minor in Adult Education. For twelve years, Sharon recorded and toured nationally with her sister, Sändra, as The Washington Sisters, and has two recordings (*Understated*, 1987; and *Take Two*, 1991). She received her tenure at Kent State University, then decided to leave and turn her varied experiences into *Tapestry Works*, a consulting company focused on diversity, adventure education and organizational development. Even though Sharon considers herself a true Ohioian, she lives and creates in western Massachusetts with her partner.

Julie L. Yetman is a twenty-six-year-old sister, daughter, lover of women and cats, feminist and lesbian who lives in St. John's, Newfoundland, with her soulmate and two rambunctious cats, Jesse and Sidney. She has a degree in Sociology and Women's Studies and is preparing for a career in Corrections. She enjoys camping, reading, animals and travel.

Lori Yetman lives in St. John's, Newfoundland, a city of about 180,000 with a relatively small lesbian community. Her home is in the suburbs with her lesbian sister and lesbian mother, their lovers, and their cats. She uses her M.A. in Women's Studies creatively, as the director of a halfway house for adult male offenders and a part-time lecturer in first year sociology at Memorial University. She misses her soulmate, who lives in Davenport, Iowa.

Lesbian Titles from Spinifex Press

This independent Australian-owned feminist publishing house ... is fast earning a reputation for producing quality literature with wide-ranging market appeal. —The Age

■ *FIGMENTS OF A MURDER* Gillian Hanscombe
A lyrical, passionate and satirical novel which crosses the boundaries of a number of genres including good literature, crime fiction, erotica and lesbian literature.
ISBN 1 875559 43 4 pb $17.95
Also by Gillian Hanscombe: *SYBIL: THE GLIDE OF HER TONGUE*
ISBN 1 875559 05 1 pb poetry $14.95

■ *COWRIE* Cathie Dunsford
Passion and desire erupt when Cowrie searches for her origins in Hawai'i.
ISBN 1 875559 28 0 pb $16.95

■ *ST SUNITI AND THE DRAGON* Suniti Namjoshi
A thoroughly modern fable.
ISBN 1 875559 18 3 pb $16.95
Also by Suniti Namjoshi: *FEMINIST FABLES*
ISBN 1 875559 19 1 pb $16.95

■ *THE FALLING WOMAN* Susan Hawthorne
"A remarkable first novel that weaves together such disparate themes as the mystery of epilepsy, love between women, and an odyssey across the Australian desert." — *Ms Magazine*
ISBN 1 875559 04 3 pb $17.95

■ *POEMS FROM THE MADHOUSE* Sandy Jeffs
NOW MILLENNIUM Deborah Staines
Two double award-winning poets. Sandy writes powerfully about schizophrenia; Deborah about the architecture of love and cities.
ISBN 1 875559 20 5 pb poetry $16.95

■ *TANSIE* Erika Kimpton
In this fiery lesbian romance Alix and Tansie explore the possibilities and limitations of love.
ISBN 1 875559 34 5 pb $16.95

SPINIFEX PRESS
504 Queensberry Street (PO Box 212), North Melbourne,
Victoria 3051, Australia
Telephone 03 9329 6088 • Facsimile 03 9329 9238 • spinifex@peg.apc.org